BETTER THAN DESTINY

BETTER THAN DESTINY

PRACTICAL SCIENCE FOR CREATING

THE LIFE YOU WANT

FREDERIC BAHNSON MD

LIONCREST
PUBLISHING

BETTER THAN DESTINY
Practical Science for Creating the Life You Want

ISBN   978-1-5445-2326-2 *Paperback*
       978-1-5445-2740-6 *Ebook*

*For Maggie, for all the challenging and wonderful
decisions we've made together—our successes,
missteps, learning, love, and ongoing journey.*

*And for Cecilia and Penelope, in the hope that you'll have as
much joy in your exploration of life as you already add to mine.*

CONTENTS

We are our choices.

—JEAN-PAUL SARTRE

INTRODUCTION

How is there freedom to choose if one does not learn how to choose?
—DAVID FOSTER WALLACE, *INFINITE JEST*

Every day, there is something you do again and again. Sometimes you do it consciously, agonizing over it for days, weeks, even months. Other times, you do it so fast you don't even realize it's happening. Sometimes it is completely inconsequential. Sometimes it entirely changes the course of your life. What is it?

Making decisions.

Throughout life, you are constantly making choices, large and small.

What shirt should I wear today?

What should I do this weekend?

Should I take the freelance gig where I can work remotely, or the office job with the retirement plan?

Should I change careers? Move cities? Start a family?

Of all the skills you have, decision-making is arguably the most important to your future happiness. Choices about your career, your relationships, and how you spend your time will shape your life. The results of small decisions add up to big impacts. A daily five-minute chat in the morning with your boss, a twenty-minute walk every day, a half hour to regularly practice a new skill... After a year, these relatively small decisions could translate to a promotion at work, improved health, and new abilities.

Decisions, big and small, are how you grow toward your desired future.

You may be intelligent, talented, and full of grit, but if you're bad at making decisions (or following through on them), it's going to be difficult to achieve your goals. This is bad news, because most of us aren't nearly as good at decision-making as we think we are, and we're not even close to as good as we could be.

YOU PROBABLY SUCK AT MAKING DECISIONS...

You probably suck at making *good* decisions. It's not personal. It's not *just* you who struggles making decisions; it's all of us.

As humans, we have many cognitive biases. These deeply ingrained, instinctual ways of thinking have served us well as a species, helping us to survive. But now that we've moved past mere survival, these biases often work against us, getting in the way of true happiness and fulfillment.

To further complicate matters, despite how important decision-making is, it hasn't made it into many school curriculums. That means it is a skill that we're not innately good at *and* that we've never been taught. Of course we struggle with it!

The whole situation can be incredibly frustrating and disheartening. You want to make good decisions, and you try to, but you don't get the results you want. You might spend years headed down one path only to eventually realize that it's not taking you where you want to go. Or you might flip-flop between options so much that you never make any forward progress. You take a few steps in one direction, feel like it's not working, then pivot and take a couple of steps in another direction. You may constantly be in motion but never travel far from your starting point.

In either case, you end up burning a lot of time and energy without getting any closer to your goals—if you're even clear on what your goals are. You know there must be a better way. You see other people who seem to have figured it out, so the information must be out there. But when you try to get this information for yourself, you'll typically find two types of resources.

First, you'll find a bunch of abstract, ineffectual self-help literature that sounds promising but doesn't deliver. While these works may contain some good ideas—and are written with the best of intentions—they typically lack actionable advice. You'll read all about the importance of finding your passion and purpose without ever learning *how* you're supposed to do that.

Second, you'll find dense scientific articles and studies. These contain nuggets of wisdom, but they're buried under jargon and references to other studies you haven't read yet. Reading through just one of these articles can take hours—and a dictionary—and at the end, you're often left with the same problem as with the self-help literature. You have no idea how to apply what you've learned to get real results in your life.

It can feel like standing on one side of a deep chasm, able to see all that you want on the other side, but with no way to get there from where you are. Considering this, it's no wonder that you may sometimes feel overwhelmed by decisions. Fear seeps in. *What if I make the wrong choice?* Paralyzed by the fear of getting it wrong, you don't make any choice at all. Which, by the way, is still a decision—one that guarantees you'll stay stuck exactly where you are.

~~~~~~

If you've struggled making decisions, you're not alone. You're not crazy or broken. You're human.

~~~~~~

If you've felt any of this, don't worry. I've been there before too—I think we *all* have. None of us is as good at decision-making as we could be, but we can each take responsibility for getting better. If you're unhappy with where you are or where you seem to be headed, you can make choices to change those things. You can choose how your future goes. You just need some knowledge and a way to put it into use. That's what this book is for.

...AND YOU CAN DEFINITELY GET BETTER

Decision-making is a skill, and like any skill, you can get better at it with practice—with one big caveat: it has to be the right kind of practice. You could spend thousands of hours throwing a football, but if you spend all those hours using the wrong form, you're never going to throw a perfect spiral. Similarly, if you want to become a better decision maker, you can't just make a bunch of decisions. You're already doing that. To improve, you need to practice making decisions *using the right strategies*.

To get better at decision-making, you need to rethink how you approach decisions and understand that making a decision is just one step in the middle of a larger process.

Before you can effectively make better decisions, you need the right mindset, and you need to understand your cognitive biases. You also need a clear vision for what you want. After all, if you don't know where you're going, how can you possibly expect to get there?

Then, when you make a deliberate decision, you need to follow through. If you're human and old enough to be reading this, you've probably failed to follow through on at least one plan or commitment you've made in the past. We've all made choices that we didn't stick with, even though we wanted to. So you also need strategies to turn your decisions into consistent action.

There's a huge body of scientific research covering all these aspects of decision-making and follow-through. This book is a distillation of that research into a practical guide for day-to-day use. It's a bridge across the metaphorical chasm.

In this book, you'll learn science-backed strategies for creating the life you want. You'll learn about:

- The importance of mindset and how to build one that sets you up for success
- Harmful cognitive biases and ways to counteract them
- Practical methods to clarify your long-term goals
- A clear process for choosing between options
- How to design an actionable plan and improve your follow-through
- How to create and use habits to reach your goals more easily and quickly
- How to stay committed to your goals even when the going gets tough
- Tips and strategies to supercharge your learning and progress

My own goal with this book is to make the information you need accessible so that you can feel empowered in your decision-making. This book is meant to be a guide you can refer back to again and again. I encourage you to read through the entire book at least once, as I've specifically organized things in such a way that understanding—and applying—the early sections will make implementing the later sections easier and more effective.

Once you have a handle on the big ideas, feel free to jump around. Need help sticking to your new workout routine?

Flip to the chapter on building habits. Feeling discouraged, as if you have no control over your life and you're never going to get better at any of this? Head back to the first chapter. Struggling to figure out what you want in life? Jump to the chapter on how to define your life and career goals.

More than anything, I want to help you create real, long-term improvement in your life. My hope is that, by the end of this book, decision-making will become an adventure for you instead of a threat. When you're presented with a range of choices, you'll feel excited instead of scared because you have the knowledge, skills, and tools to navigate your way forward. Not only will you start making better decisions—you'll enjoy the process and feel more comfortable creating the life of your dreams.

MY DECISION-MAKING JOURNEY

At this point, you might be thinking, "This all sounds great, but why should I listen to *you*?" It's a fair question. Your time is valuable. If I'm asking you to spend some of it reading this book, I should know what I'm talking about.

I do have several credentials that look good on my résumé. I have a degree in physics and am a practicing general surgeon, whose surgical training included experience at LA County Trauma Center. I am a fellow of the American College of Surgeons. I am an advisor to and also served as the Chief Medical Officer for Macro-Eyes, an artificial intelligence company working on global public health. This background has allowed me to understand and translate the science of decision-making into practical, results-focused strategies, which I've refined through my personal and executive coaching practice.

Honestly, that last paragraph makes me a bit uncomfortable. Partly because *any* sort of self-promotion makes me uncomfortable, but also because it gives a false impression that my life has been a single successful plan that has fit neatly together in a way that would have made sense from the start. That's definitely not how it happened. The truth is that I had a lot of messy years before reaching where I am today. And it's those messy years, not my résumé, that really make me qualified to write this book.

I didn't start out thinking I'd be a doctor or coach. I grew up on a farm, without a lot of money and in a town a lot of people never left. We definitely weren't wealthy, but my parents always stressed the importance of education. As part of leaving the farm and our small town, I attended Reed College, where I got my physics degree.

It wasn't until I was nearly done with college that a hard truth sunk in for me: there's not a lot of demand for physicists. If I wanted to "do physics," I'd have to get an advanced degree and go into academia, which I wasn't interested in. I had loans, and I needed a job of some kind. I pivoted into engineering and found work in research and development making electron microscopes.

It didn't take long for me to become unhappy with my work. I did enjoy the tinkering and intellectual problems of the job, and I liked the people I worked with. But the nonstop, often pointless meetings bothered me, and I didn't like the way the sales process drove the development process. People who had been there for decades were frustrated with all the same stuff I was, and I could see how dissatisfied many of them were. Worst of all, I struggled to find meaning in my work. Many people find their engineering jobs very fulfilling, but for me, something was missing.

I thought maybe it was just the company, so I found a different engineering job at a different company. I promptly ran into the same issues. I enjoyed the tinkering, I liked the people, but I hated the overall work environment.

Let's recap my big decisions up to that point:

Majoring in physics? Interesting and educational but didn't get me where I wanted to go.

Pivoting to engineering? Same problem.

Quitting one engineering job only to move to another with the same issues? All right, it's starting to look like I make *really* bad decisions. *Why am I writing a book on this again?*

Here's the thing: at that second engineering job, I made an important mental shift. I decided that, instead of just running away from the things I didn't like, I needed to figure out what I was running toward. I came up with several options: opening a martial arts gym, going back to school for environmental science, getting into robotics, or going into medicine.

This is where my education on decision-making kicked into high gear.

I didn't want to keep jumping from one dissatisfying job to another, so I read everything I could about decision-making. I pored through research articles, books, and countless pieces on the web.

For the first time, I understood *how* to make better decisions. As I learned—about decision-making and about myself—I weighed my options and eventually chose medicine. That decision has turned out very well. Medicine is not right for everyone, but it was right for *me*. It helped me create the fulfillment and meaning that had been missing for me in my engineering roles, and it proved to me how important decision-making is to our happiness.

STANDING AT THE FEET OF GIANTS

Of course, I wasn't naive enough to think that a single good decision meant I was suddenly a master. I continued researching decision-making and grew more and more fascinated with the topic. And the more I read, the more I felt something was missing.

On the self-help side, the advice felt too vague. On the science side, researchers rarely seemed to offer practical suggestions. They consistently said, "More research is needed." From a scientist's perspective, I understood the academic hesitancy to commit, but as a person wanting to get better at making decisions, it was incredibly unhelpful. If you're trying to choose a career, set your kids up for success, or build long-term habits that stick, you don't have time to wait twenty years for the results of the next long-term study. You need tools you can use—*now*.

I am fortunate because my science background sets me up to interpret and apply the most impactful and current research across my life. And it gets results.

At times, I feel a little guilty, though. It sometimes feels like I have this secret key to life, and it isn't fair. *Everyone* deserves to have access to this knowledge, not just those who have spent years working through journal articles and translating the theory into practice. Because of this, I began working as a personal and executive coach, to share what I'd learned. After seeing the very real impact these principles and strategies can have on people's lives, I want to share these ideas with even more people—thus this book.

On the surface, it might seem strange for a doctor to become a coach. But coaching, much like medicine, is often about helping people better understand what is already happening to them and translating available knowledge in a way that helps them move forward. Many of my duties in the medical profession also revolve around being a translator. In my day-to-day work as a surgeon, I must simplify and break down the science for my patients and help them understand, make, and follow through on important decisions. Within the health system where I work, I help with data analytics, functioning as a translator between the data analysts and scientists on one side and the physicians and medical directors on the other. At Macro-Eyes too, I spent a lot of time serving as a bridge between the machine learning folks building decision support tools and the doctors who use those tools to help themselves and their patients make better decisions.

With my coaching and in this book, I'm again serving as a translator, now with the science of decision-making. At this point, I've read hundreds of research articles and dozens of related books, and I've tested these ideas in my own life as well as with clients and patients. With this book, I am translating that information into one neatly packaged, easy-to-understand, practical resource.

One way to think about it is that we're all navigating our way through this dense jungle of our lives with no premade path, and we can only see a short distance in front of us. In this jungle with us is a tribe of giants, each giant looking in a different direction. These giants are the different researchers who have uncovered important truths and discoveries about decision-making, planning, and human happiness and well-being. They each can see in great detail and for great distance, but only along a very narrow arc of the landscape.

Metaphorically, I am standing not on the shoulders of these giants, but at their feet. I'm down in the jungle with you, able to understand the very real challenges you're facing, and I've also become pretty good at understanding these giants and getting a good picture of what they see. Because of this, instead of getting the perspective of a single giant, who can see in only one direction, I can offer you a complete map of the jungle. I'm pulling out the practical points from the knowledge of a whole tribe of giants, integrating them into a single resource for navigating the jungle of your day-to-day life.

Every time you need to make a decision, you don't want to pull out twenty different books or struggle through a stack of research articles to get the information you need. You want a framework and guide that is broad and easy to apply across the vast majority of circumstances. That's what I seek to provide with this book.

You've already made one great decision in picking up this book. If you're ready to make progress toward the future you want, it's time for your next great decision of many to come: turn the page.

CHAPTER 1

——

YOU HAVE NO DESTINY, AND THAT'S A GOOD THING

Your own path you make with every step you take. That's why it's your path.

—JOSEPH CAMPBELL

There are over seven billion people in the world. When I wanted to find just one to share the rest of my life with, I was focused on a single gender within my general age range. That narrowed my focus to something still over a billion people.

I'm happily married now, despite those seemingly astronomical odds. Even winning the lottery seems more likely, with chances of one in several million. Clearly, I'm lucky, but is that all there is to it? How did my wife, Margarita, and I come to be together?

There were many moments where if one thing were slightly different, our paths never would have crossed. If we didn't both attend the same college, if we weren't both single at the time, if we hadn't both been out playing volleyball with mutual friends…if, if, if, if, if.

Some people would say it was fate. So many circumstances had to align perfectly just for us to meet, and even more factors—family and friends, interests, values—had to line up for things to work out. It *had* to be destiny…right?

Wrong. It was our choices.

YOU HAVE NO DESTINY

First off, we have to get one thing out of the way. It hurts, but it's got to be said, and understood: you have no destiny.

That's actually a good thing. I'm not saying you have no future. I'm saying that your future is not predetermined. You are not destined for wild success, nor are you destined for tragic failure.

~~~~~

You get to choose your future.

~~~~~

I'm also not saying that you have control over everything. There is plenty in life that we don't get to choose—where we're born, who our birth parents are, our race, the socioeconomic class we're raised in, and more. Chance plays a role in the trajectory of our lives, but we get to choose what we do with the chances that come our way.

Following college, for instance, Margarita had a career opportunity in Chicago, while I had to stay in Portland. We had both made our commitments before our relationship got serious. Because of previous experiences with long-distance relationships (which clearly hadn't worked out), we decided to break up. Shortly after graduation, we went our separate ways, and I was unhappy.

If I was a true believer in destiny, I might have simply accepted this and said, "We weren't meant to be." Fortunately, I did not have such a destiny mindset. I recognized this situation for what it was: not fate, but a decision. I fulfilled my prior obligation in Portland, then chose to find freelance and temp work in Chicago. It was mindless grunt work, like alphabetizing files for a hotel chain, but it gave Margarita and me the chance to continue our relationship.

We got back together, and the rest is history—a history built by thousands of decisions. Some of the decisions were big: deciding to get married, to have kids, to work through our disagreements and challenges. And some were smaller: deciding to take her on a date to her favorite restaurant, to call and chat even after an exhausting day at work, to move. When you add all those decisions up, you realize that we are together not because of destiny, but because we chose to be. If you ask me, that's even more romantic than the concept of fate and soulmates. We chose this, and we built it.

You might be thinking, "But I *like* having a destiny." Destiny makes us feel special. It can give us hope, promising a brighter future even when our present is not so great. It's time for another hard truth: if all you do is wish for—or expect—a brighter future, you'll never actually achieve it. If you really want a brighter future, *you* have to make it happen. Instead of destiny, you need goals to work toward.

Maybe you're on the other side of the spectrum and are thinking, "I know I don't have a destiny. All that 'chosen one' stuff is for books and movies." I agree, but it's important to understand that a destiny mindset can be more subtle than that. Believing in destiny can mean believing there is something you are *meant* to do or be. For most of us, a destiny mindset shows up in expectations and assumptions. For instance, maybe you assume you will go to college, follow a certain career path, live in a certain place, or have children, not because you've consciously made choices to do so, but because it's what you believe you "should" do or what you've always expected you would do.

One of the biggest places this subtle destiny mindset shows up is the idea of purpose.

YOU DON'T HAVE TO FIND ONE TRUE PURPOSE EITHER

Destiny is the assumption that there's one singular thing that's right for you, now and forever. If you believe you have *one* grand, deep purpose that you have to discover in life, you believe in destiny, whether you call it that or not.

Purpose is a popular topic in self-help advice. The way some talk about it, it's the most important thing in life, as if failing to find your one true purpose dooms you to only experience superficial, short-term happiness and not deeper fulfillment or sustainable well-being.

The result is that we put way too much pressure on ourselves to find our destined purpose. When that purpose isn't immediately apparent, we get frustrated and beat ourselves up. "Why can't I figure this out?" we ask. "Shouldn't it be obvious?"

The answer is no, it's not always obvious, because purpose isn't found. It's *created*. Later in this book, we'll talk about how the things that develop into our passions (which can later evolve into purpose) are the things we try and, in doing so, learn more about. Basically, the more we do something, the more interested in and passionate about it we become. The more passionate we are about something, the more likely we are to be able to identify a purpose in it that is meaningful to us. The reverse is also true. If we choose to focus on the purpose of a pursuit, we are much more likely to develop a passion for it, starting a positive loop that creates an even deeper sense of purpose.

Because purpose is created, there's no limit to the number of purposes you can work toward in your life. In all likelihood, you will find many ways to serve different purposes at different times in your life.

~~~~~

You will change and grow—probably more than you expect—and your passions and purpose may evolve as well.

~~~~~

Imagine yourself ten years from now. Maybe you'll have a new favorite band or get a promotion within your industry. Perhaps you'll be living somewhere else or will have made new friends. But internally, in terms of your core values, personality, and likes and dislikes, how much do you think you'll change? Try to put a number on it. On a scale of 0 to 10, with 0 being no change at all and 10 being a complete 180 on your values, personality, and preferences, how much do you think you'll change in the next ten years?

Now look back at yourself ten years ago. I'm guessing you were a pretty different person back then, and you can probably identify a lot of ways you've changed, both big and small. Again, try to put a number on it: on a scale of 0 to 10, how much have you changed over the past ten years, in terms of your core values, personality, and preferences?

Now compare your numbers. If you're like most people, your first number will be lower than your second. This is something called the end-of-history illusion. At any given moment in time, we think we're living at the end of our personal development. Looking back, we can see how we've experienced significant growth, but looking forward, we don't expect to change too much more. "Yes, I've grown a lot," we think, "and now I have become who I *am*."

To be fair, there is *some* truth to this. As we age, our rate of change does slow down. But—and this is a big *but*—it doesn't drop nearly as much as we think it will. Scientific studies have shown that, at all ages, we significantly underestimate the growth we will experience over the next ten years.[1] So much so, in fact, that the amount eighteen-year-olds *predict* they will change in a decade is how much fifty-year-olds *actually* change over a decade.

---

1   Jordi Quoidbach, Daniel T. Gilbert, and Timothy D. Wilson, "The End of History Illusion," *Science* 339, no. 6115 (2013): 96–98.

As Dan Gilbert, one of the key researchers behind explaining the end-of-history illusion, says, "Human beings are works in progress that mistakenly think they're finished."[2] You are not who you will be in the future. So it makes sense that you will discover new meaning and purpose throughout life. This doesn't mean your previous purposes were wrong; it just means you've grown.

HOW YOU THINK MATTERS: FIXED MINDSET VERSUS GROWTH MINDSET

So you have choices, not a destiny, and you will create purpose*s*, not find *a* purpose. Is this anything more than semantics? Is it really that big of a deal to talk about your destiny and purpose, as long as you keep in the back of your mind that you actually have to work toward your future and may choose to work toward more than one purpose?

Well, yeah. As you will see throughout this book, details matter.

~~~~~

A lot of psychology and human behavioral research has revealed that how we think about our situation affects how we behave in that situation.

~~~~~

<hr />

2   Dan Gilbert, "The Psychology of Your Future Self," TED, March 2014, https://www.ted.com/talks/ dan_gilbert_the_psychology_of_your_future_self. This TED Talk is a great, quick breakdown of the end-of-history illusion if you'd like to learn more.

In particular, whether you have a *fixed mindset* or a *growth mindset* will have a huge impact on your outcomes, and language plays a big role in which of those mindsets you have.

In 2006, drawing on three decades of her own research and the research of many others, psychologist Carol Dweck, PhD, introduced the general public to these ideas with her book *Mindset*.[3] Dweck summarizes the fixed mindset as "believing that your qualities are carved in stone." A person with a fixed mindset believes "you have only a certain amount of intelligence, a certain personality, and a certain moral character."

In contrast, the growth mindset is "based on the belief that your basic qualities are things you can cultivate through your efforts, your strategies, and help from others." Someone with a growth mindset believes that "although people may differ in every which way—in their initial talents and aptitudes, interests, or temperaments—everyone can change and grow through application and experience."

This simple difference in mindset can affect a number of different life outcomes. Dweck's and others' research has shown correlations between a growth mindset and success in school, employment, leadership positions, sports, and relationships. For instance, students with a growth mindset are more likely to improve their grades at times when people with a fixed mindset lose ground. A growth mindset also makes people more likely to move up in the hierarchy of their workplace, and leaders who have a growth mindset not only toward themselves but toward their team members tend to provide more effective coaching and have more successful teams.

---

3   Carol S. Dweck, *Mindset: The New Psychology of Success* (New York: Random House, 2006).

These links make sense. If you believe that your own capabilities (and those of people around you) are basically set as they are, then you are less likely to take risks that might expose any of your own weaknesses. On the other hand, if you believe you and those around you can grow, you tend to view your own (current) deficiencies as opportunities to learn rather than fixed traits to be ashamed of and hidden. Thus, while a fixed mindset causes you to avoid challenges, a growth mindset pushes you to seek them out and persevere despite difficulties. With a growth mindset, you're also more likely to ask for help when you need it, and you can bounce back from losses and failures more quickly.

Believing in destiny creates a fixed mindset about your whole life. The language is even shared—destiny is a *fixed* future. Based on the research about mindset, if you believe in destiny, you are more likely to avoid challenges rather than face them. You are also less likely to ask for help; more likely to hide your failures and blame others rather than learn, grow, and collaborate; and more likely to avoid work rather than seek out new opportunities.

So if you take away only one thing from this book, let it be this: neither your traits nor your future are fixed. In any area of your life, you can grow and get better, including getting better at making decisions.

WHICH MINDSET DO YOU HAVE?

Clearly, mindset is important, so how can you tell which mindset you have? It's actually a spectrum, as opposed to a clear black-and-white distinction. You can measure where you fall on the sliding scale of fixed-to-growth mindset by asking how much you agree or disagree with statements such as:

1. You have a certain level of intelligence (or artistic talent, athletic ability, social skill, etc.), and you can't change it much.
2. No matter your initial aptitudes, you can always significantly change your skills and traits.
3. You are a certain kind of person, and you can't really change that.
4. You can always change substantially, even basic things about the kind of person you are.
5. Talent is something you're born with, not something you can develop.
6. If you practice something for long enough, you can develop a talent for it.

If you agree with the odd-number statements (#1, #3, and #5), you tend toward a fixed mindset. If you agree with the even-number statements (#2, #4, and #6), you lean toward a growth mindset.

Another good way to identify a fixed mindset in action is to look out for absolute statements:

- "I am bad at x."
- "I am good at y."
- "I will never get better at this."
- "I will always struggle with _____."

Also consider how you react to mistakes and failures. If a mistake or failure makes you think you're not smart or talented, you're thinking with a fixed mindset. If, on the other hand, you see mistakes and failures as learning opportunities, you're working with a growth mindset.

Most likely, you will not have just one mindset or the other. Nearly all of us have a growth mindset in some areas of our life and a fixed mindset in others. You may think, "I have zero musical talent and can never be a musician" and simultaneously think, "I don't know any Spanish, but I can learn." Sometimes the discrepancy in mindset is due to external factors. For instance, studies have shown that stereotypes—like the idea that girls are bad at math—can also play a role in our mindset toward certain activities. Some differences in mindset might be due to conditioning you received at a young age. As a child, if teachers and adults in your life routinely told you, "You're so smart!", you may have developed a fixed mindset about your intelligence, believing it to be an innate part of you—something you were born with—as opposed to something to be cultivated through hard work. Simultaneously, if you had a soccer coach who emphasized the importance of practice and praised you for how hard you worked, you may have developed a growth mindset around your athletic ability.

Take some time to evaluate your mindset in different areas of your life. Where do you have a growth mindset, and where do you have a fixed mindset?

Fixed Mindset

With a fixed mindset, you...

Believe skills, intelligence, and talent are traits that you have a certain —fixed— amount of	**Beliefs**
Avoid challenges because they risk exposing your weaknesses	**Challenges**
Give up easily in the face of challenges, believing that having to work hard means you're not good enough	**Effort**
Take mistakes and failures to mean you are a failure	**Mistakes**
Blame setbacks on others	
Take feedback personally and get defensive	**Feedback**
Feel threatened by the success of others	**Success of Others**

All these things reinforce a deterministic view of the world and your own future.

Growth Mindset

With a growth mindset, you...

Beliefs	Understand that skills, intelligence, and talent can be developed
Challenges	Seek challenges and the opportunities they provide to learn and grow
Effort	Persist in the face of challenges, believing effort helps you develop new skills and is the pathway to mastery
Mistakes	View mistakes and failures as opportunities to learn
	Reflect on setbacks and use them as lessons
Feedback	Appreciate feedback as something useful to learn from
Success of Others	Find inspiration and lessons in the success of others

All of these things open up increased feelings of free will and agency in your own future.

HOW TO CHANGE YOUR MINDSET

Let's say you've identified that you have a fixed mindset, at least in some area of your life. No worries—Dweck and other researchers have shown that we can learn how to change our mindsets. In other words, the research supports having a growth mindset *about your mindset!*

Understanding the two mindsets is a great first step, but simply being aware isn't enough. I made a promise in the introduction to provide you with not just theory but also practical advice to make a real difference in your life. So how can you grow your mindset? You can consciously work to understand and reinforce your own knowledge: practice makes us better, hard work has rewards, and who we are and what we are capable of can change—and grow.

CHANGE YOUR LANGUAGE

One of the easiest ways to change your mindset is to change your language. The research on mindset has highlighted that this simple psychological trick can move us into, or out of, a growth mindset.

In one experiment, two sets of children were given the same puzzle task.[4] Then the two groups were given subtly different

---

4   C. M. Mueller and C. S. Dweck, "Praise for Intelligence Can Undermine Children's Motivation and Performance," *Journal of Personal and Social Psychology* 75, no. 1 (1998): 33–52.

feedback. One group was praised for how *smart* they were (a fixed trait). The other was praised for how *hard they worked* on the first puzzles (an attribute of growth).

This subtle difference in language changed how the groups behaved. The "smart" group behaved in a fixed-mindset way. When offered a choice for the next task, they deliberately chose easier puzzles. The "hard work" group was much more likely to choose harder puzzles. Subsequent interviews with the children and further related experiments reinforced the findings. The children praised for being smart wanted to avoid challenges that might expose them as not as smart, while the children praised for working hard sought out challenges that could help them learn and grow.

Experiments in college students and working adults in different scenarios have similar findings. In one study, researchers worked with students from a two-semester statistics course in college.[5] They taught students the mindset theories and used mindfulness exercises to reinforce a growth mindset with statements like: "I am capable of understanding math" and "I expect to make mistakes today and then learn from those mistakes." These simple changes decreased students' anxiety related to math, increased their feeling that they could learn and do math, and ultimately resulted in higher grades.

What these experiments demonstrate is that language *does* matter. Your mindset may bias you toward certain language, but you can flip that around. You can change your mindset

---

5   Tashana S. Samuel and Jared Warner, "'I Can Math!': Reducing Math Anxiety and Increasing Math Self-Efficacy Using a Mindfulness and Growth Mindset-Based Intervention in First-Year Students," *Community College Journal of Research and Practice* 45, no. 3 (2021): 205–22.

by deliberately changing your word choice—in your own mind and outside your head.

WATCH OUT FOR RED FLAGS AND YOUR TRIGGERS

The trick to this strategy is knowing *when* you need to change your language. That means learning to recognize red flags and identify the triggers that send you into a fixed mindset.

The red flags are those absolute statements we talked about earlier: "I am good at _____" and "I am bad at _____." Anytime you are approaching something from that framework, you're probably in a fixed mindset. It's important to recognize both the positive and negative forms of these statements. While saying or thinking "I am good at _____" *seems* like a positive thing, you're still looking at that skill or trait as something fixed. That will hinder your growth and keep you from reaching your full potential. You don't want to *be good*; you want to *get better*. Instead of "I am good at _____," acknowledge that "I've gotten better and better at _____." It may be true that you're good at something, but it probably wasn't always true. Recognizing your past growth will remind you, when you're struggling with something else, that you've been a beginner before and improved over time. It will also reinforce that no matter how good you are, you may have opportunities to get even better.

You can also watch out for the triggers that take you from a growth mindset to a fixed mindset. Three of the most common triggers are criticism, struggle, and comparison to others' success.

When someone criticizes you, what's your initial gut reaction?

Do you think there's something you can work on? Or do you think your bad performance translates into a bad part of your identity? "I'm terrible." "I'm a complete failure." If your default reaction is a fixed mindset, that's okay. The key is to recognize what's happening and then shift yourself back into a growth mindset. Remind yourself of these simple facts: practice works, and people learn. You're a person—you'll learn, and you'll get better with practice. The more you work on shifting your mindset, the more you'll train yourself to default to a growth mindset instead of a fixed mindset.

When you have to work hard at a task, how does it make you feel? Does it trigger you to think you must not be good at the task? Do you get frustrated and discouraged? Or do you think, "This is difficult, so I must be developing a skill?" Again, you might not be able to control your split-second reaction—at least at first—but the quicker you recognize it and remind yourself of the benefits of learning from challenges, the quicker you'll get back to a growth mindset and an openness to taking opportunities to improve and grow.

Finally, how do you feel when you see other people succeed? Does it inspire you to keep practicing and working? Or do you think, "I'll never be as good as them, so why bother trying?" It might help to consider the amount of effort it took them to succeed. We'll talk more about this later when we discuss grit, but successful people typically worked harder to build their successes than we want to give them credit for.

Stay on the lookout for those times and areas of your life in which you habitually fall into a fixed mindset. Whenever you do recognize a fixed mindset, try to identify what triggered it. The more you can identify the root causes of your fixed mindset, the quicker you'll be able to train yourself to pop back into a growth mindset.

REFRAME FAILURE

I'm sure you've heard lots of motivational sayings about failure. "Fall down seven times, get up eight." "You only fail when you stop trying." "You learn more from failure than success." It's easy to dismiss such aphorisms as unrealistic and overly peppy, but they hold valuable truths. Learning to reframe failure is an important part of a growth mindset.

A simple reframing strategy is to think of life as a series of experiments. You may go into a certain project—whether it's learning a new skill, switching careers, or whatever—with a hypothesis. You have a guess for what's going to happen. And if the experiment doesn't prove your hypothesis, that doesn't mean the experiment was a failure. It means you now have more information. You can create a more informed hypothesis, which will allow you to design better experiments in the future. Over time, this process of growth is more important than the results of any one experiment.

Too often, we visualize the ideal outcome of what we're working on, and we deem any outcome that doesn't match that ideal a failure. In many cases, our "failures" are not as bad as we feel they are; they just don't match our ideal outcome. Even in the worst-case scenario, when a particular effort completely falls flat, you have important information about what *not* to do in the future.

Also remember that failures (and criticisms) are not a reflection of *you* as a person, but of your *particular attempt* at a task. If you bake a batch of cookies that taste terrible, it doesn't mean you're a bad human, or even a bad baker. It simply means this particular recipe turned out poorly this time.

Reframing failures as learning opportunities shifts your focus to continual improvement and growth. And in the long run, growing will provide you more opportunities, and more happiness, than waiting for your destiny ever would.

DECISIONS ARE BETTER THAN DESTINY

Theoretically, you could go through life without making conscious decisions unless forced to. You could let life happen to you, waiting for your destiny to manifest. But you don't want to do that. I know, because there is something fundamental we all share as humans.

Monk and author David Steindl-Rast puts it like this:

> There is something you know about me, something very personal, and there is something I know about every one of you and that's very central to your concerns. There is something that we know about everyone we meet anywhere in the world, on the street, that is the very mainspring of whatever they do and whatever they put up with. And that is that all of us want to be happy.[6]

How we define happiness and what it means to us may differ from person to person. Some people may call it fulfillment or life satisfaction. Others may think of it as deep contentment.

---

6   David Steindl-Rast, "Want to Be Happy? Be Grateful," TEDGlobal, June 2013, https://www.ted.com/talks/david_steindl_rast_want_to_be_happy_be_grateful.

We may find it in our families, our careers, our communities, or our hobbies. But the bottom line is that we all want to be happy.

Because your future isn't fixed, your ability to make better decisions is your ability to make a better future for yourself, to find and create your happiness. A growth mindset—which you can develop by changing your language, recognizing red flags and identifying your triggers, and reframing failure—is your first step to learning how to make better decisions.

So no, you don't have a destiny, but you have something better: you have choices. You get to choose what you do with your time, what goals to pursue and how to pursue them, and who you build a life with.

You get the picture—your choices, and how you approach them, will have a big effect on your life. This makes sense to a lot of us, and yet, in a surprising number of situations, we continue to default to choosing not to decide. In the next chapter, we'll unpack why we do this and why it may be the worst choice you can make.

CHAPTER 2

THE WORST DECISION YOU CAN MAKE

Whatever you decide, don't let it be because you don't think you have a choice.

—HANNAH HARRINGTON, *SAVING JUNE*

One day I walked into the living room to find my older daughter crying on the couch. I was concerned, as any parent would be. "What's going on?" I asked, sitting down with her.

"I don't want to do gymnastics anymore," she told me.

"All right," I said. "Why does that make you so sad?"

"I'm afraid I'm disappointing you guys," she said, which broke my heart a little.

I wasn't disappointed with her decision to stop gymnastics; I was surprised. My daughter had done competitive gymnastics for many years. It's a fairly all-consuming sport, requiring many hours of practice every week and a lot of sacrifices.

Due to her hours at the gym, she missed out on many activities—school sports, extracurricular activities, evening outings, weekend sleepovers, family travel.

She loved gymnastics, though, and she was always the driver for doing more. Occasionally, she'd ask about doing some other activity, like Ultimate Frisbee or a service trip. My wife and I would tell her we fully supported her doing other activities, but we'd point out that they overlapped with gymnastics. "You have to do less gymnastics if you want to do that—you can't be in both places at the same time." For years, considering activity after activity, my daughter would immediately respond with some version of "Then no. I don't want to do less gym."

It was the summer after eighth grade when she told me she wanted to quit. That season had started out challenging for her, but after a few months, mentally and competitively, she was killing it. With her persistence and hard work, along with some great coaches, she won at state and qualified for Western Nationals, the highest level of competition for Level 9 gymnasts. Division I colleges recruit from Level 9, 10, and Elite in gymnastics, so she was already competing at a level to get college attention. We had started thinking about filtering colleges based on prospects for a Division I gymnastics scholarship. She ended up doing well at Westerns and felt good about her performance. Only a few weeks later, she was telling us she wanted to be done.

I asked whether she had any regrets and why she'd decided to quit. In gymnastics, a lot of horrible things can go on behind the scenes that could be a reason why a girl would want to get out of the sport. I wanted to make sure there wasn't something we had missed.

She gave me a surprisingly articulate and mature response for her age. "I don't regret having done gymnastics," she told me. "But it's not worth it anymore. There are too many other things I want to do, and I don't love it enough anymore to make it worth not getting to do those other things."

So we did a big pivot. With gymnastics out of the picture, she was able to take a trip with a service organization to Panama, where she made new friends, did service work she was proud of, and learned a lot more Spanish. She was also able to join a couple of school sports, including Ultimate Frisbee. She was able to go bowling and to movie nights and other normal social events with her friends from school. And we were able to start taking more trips together as a family.

It's ironic that she thought she was letting us down, because it was one of my proudest moments as a parent. In quitting gymnastics, my daughter did something that many adults struggle to do: she recognized a big opportunity cost and decided to make a change.

THE PROBLEM WITH NOT DECIDING: OPPORTUNITY COST

The number one decision-making mistake is not making a conscious decision. Despite this, we often stick with the status quo, letting things go on as they always have, without realizing that not deciding is its own kind of choice with significant opportunity costs.

Opportunity cost is the lost value of the things you *can't* do because of the time, money, and resources spent on what you *are* doing. There are both explicit and implicit opportunity costs. With explicit opportunity costs, if you get one thing, you can't get the other, while implicit opportunity costs are lost opportunities to gain additional value because of other choices.

Let's say you have $12,000 and spend it all on a gold bathtub. The explicit opportunity cost is that now you can't spend that money on something else—like first-class tickets to Hawaii or a used electric car. The implicit opportunity cost is that you can't use that money to make more money or generate other value on top of the initial $12,000. For instance, if you invested the money, you could perhaps make an additional $1,000 over time. That $1,000 is an implicit opportunity cost. You didn't lose that $1,000 by buying the tub (or the Hawaii vacation or the electric car), but you lost the opportunity to make the extra money.

My daughter's story is full of both explicit and implicit opportunity costs. In choosing to commit to gymnastics, she explicitly missed out on several seasons of Ultimate Frisbee and quite a few movie nights and bowling trips. Those events would have been opportunities to expand or deepen her friendships outside of the gym. Missing out on those opportunities for growth was an implicit cost of her commitment to gym practice. For many years, those opportunity costs were worth it to her, because she loved gymnastics so much—her teammates, her coaches, learning new skills, traveling to competitions. But, like all of us, she grew and changed.

Leaving gymnastics wasn't an easy decision for her. She didn't hate gymnastics. She didn't quit because she'd had a bad week or a bad season or because she had a competition coming up and didn't want to do the extra practice. The opportunity costs simply weren't worth it to her anymore.

Of course, quitting gymnastics also had opportunity costs. She doesn't see her gymnastics friends as much now. There are new skills she'll never get to learn and competitions she'll never get to travel to. She no longer has a shot at a gymnastics scholarship, and she'll never be on a high-level college gymnastics team.

~~~~~~

Whether we stick with the status quo or try something new, there are always opportunity costs.

~~~~~~

These types of trade-offs are real for all of us. We can't be everywhere and do all things at all times. While we are considering how this affects our decisions and our lives, there is an important psychological reality to keep in mind: we are often quite good at considering the opportunity costs of making a big change, but we are not as good at considering the opportunity costs of *not* making the change.

FEAR: WHY WE DON'T DECIDE

Like many human behaviors, our tendency to not decide is related to fear. We're afraid of losing what we currently have. We're afraid we'll make the wrong choice and later regret it. We're afraid of the unknown. These fears cause us to overestimate the opportunity costs of making a change and underestimate the opportunity costs of *not* making the change.

Our current reality is both familiar and concrete. If you're considering changing jobs, it is relatively easy to list a lot of downsides—loss of financial stability, changes in your social groups, a possible move away from a place you are comfortable living. Your current income, your current social group, your current home—you don't have to be particularly imaginative to picture giving these things up.

What takes a lot more imagination is picturing the things that would replace your current reality. What would your new job actually be like? You'd hopefully have a vague sense before you take it, but it is nothing like the detail with which you understand and can picture your current job. What new friends would you make? What would living in the new place be like? Same thing—easy to imagine in broad strokes, but nothing like the detail with which you can think about your current day-to-day life.

Taking this a step further, it is even harder to consider the implicit costs of not making a change. What opportunities for growth, new experiences, and greater happiness will you pass up by staying at a job you hate?

How possible—and desirable—an imaginary future seems to us is strongly related to the level of detail in our imagination of that future. The things we expect to give up by making a change are things we experience regularly. They are concrete and detailed in our mind, and so they seem more real than the things we stand to gain in making a change. We can't understand gains we haven't gotten yet in nearly the same way, so it is easy to discount them and pay less attention to them. Add to this the fact that the idea of losing something we already have is much harder to stomach than losing something we *could* have, and you have a strong bias against trying something new.

On top of this, the opportunity for regret seems bigger when we make a change. If we choose change and it doesn't turn out well, we blame ourselves. It was our action—our choice—that caused us pain. In contrast, if we don't do anything, it's not that hard to mentally and emotionally absolve ourselves of responsibility. We tell ourselves that if we're not as happy as we could be, it's not our fault. That's just how our life is. And we end up passively coasting along.

We do this frequently, and at our own peril. If you talk to people later in life about what they regret, the vast majority talk not about choices they made or actions they took. They talk about those things they *didn't* do or that they waited too long to do.

~~~~~

Time and time again, we fear regretting our choices, but what we actually end up regretting, time and time again, is the changes we didn't make, and the chances we didn't take.

~~~~~

We miss a lot of opportunities because we fail to even consider they're out there. We assume that something we can't be sure of must be less meaningful than something we already have, even if what we already have doesn't seem that great. And it's not just fear to blame. Our brains have evolved to think this way. In addition to our fear, many cognitive biases affect how we think about change. Two powerful and common biases that are worth learning about are the sunk cost fallacy and the status quo bias.

THE SUNK COST FALLACY: WHY IT'S SO HARD TO CHANGE COURSE

Have you ever started a movie, realized thirty minutes in that you didn't really like it, but continued watching anyway?

Have you ever been involved in a work project that clearly wasn't going to achieve what it was supposed to, but the team kept pushing ahead with it anyway?

Have you ever been unhappy with your career, a relationship, or some other aspect of your life but thought, *I've already put in so much time/effort/money, I might as well stick with it*?

If so, you've experienced the sunk cost fallacy.

WHAT IT IS, AND WHY WE DO IT

The sunk cost fallacy is our tendency to pour more resources into something—more time, money, and effort—because of what we have already put into it, rather than what we expect to get in return. The error comes from thinking that what we have put in so far has less value if we change paths, but more value if we continue on the path we're already on. Essentially, we don't want the time, money, and effort we've already spent to be "wasted." We feel that, if we persist on the path we're already on, this will somehow justify the resources we've already put in, but if we switch paths those already spent resources are somehow "more lost" or "more wasted."

Many studies document the existence and effects of the sunk cost fallacy.[7] One of the most interesting to me compared two species of monkey.[8] In this study, capuchin and rhesus monkeys learned to persist in a task to earn a reward. The monkeys, who learned the tasks easily, then failed to adjust their strategy even when conditions changed and it would clearly be better for the monkey to "give up" on one task and move on to the next. Through carefully controlling the conditions, the researchers discovered that while both species of monkeys displayed the sunk cost fallacy, one species showed it even more than the other. Interestingly, the two species have different feeding strategies in the wild. The rhesus monkeys, whose feeding strategy requires more persistence, were also the monkeys that were more likely to fall into the sunk cost fallacy.

What this and other studies suggest is that the sunk cost fallacy has useful roots. It makes sense from an evolutionary perspective. Persistence does often pay off. If you're trying to dig termites out of a tree with a stick, you might not get any

7   See H. R. Arkes and C. Blumer, "The Psychology of Sunk Costs," *Organizational Behavior and Human Decision Processes* 35 (1985): 124–40; H. Garland and S. Newport, "Effects of Absolute and Relative Sunk Costs on the Decision to Persist with a Course of Action," *Organizational Behavior and Human Decision Processes* 48 (1991): 55–69; and H. Moon, "Looking Forward and Looking Back: Integrating Completion and Sunk-Cost Effects within an Escalation-of-Commitment Progress Decision," *Journal of Applied Psychology* 86 (2001): 104–13.

8   J. Watzek and S. F. Brosnan, "Capuchin and Rhesus Monkeys Show Sunk Cost Effects in a Psychomotor Task," *Scientific Reports* 10, no. 20396 (2020).

on the first try. If you try it a few more times, though, you may get some termites, and now you have more food and are more likely to survive than if you'd given up after the first try.

In many ways, it's helpful that we have evolved to be persistent. Persistence helps us develop tools, build civilizations, and continue to discover new innovations from generation to generation. But it's not the right approach for every situation. It's only appropriate when what we're persisting toward is something we actually still want. The sunk cost fallacy is a time when persistence makes us miss the mark and tricks us to waste even more resources instead of getting the most out of them.

HOW IT IMPACTS DECISION-MAKING

In decision-making, the sunk cost fallacy means we're biased to stick with what we've already invested in, even if it's not the best option for us in the future. Often, the result is that we dump in even more time, money, and effort, without getting any of the things we really want.

Let's use the example of a bad movie. You go to the theater, pay $10 for your ticket and perhaps another $15 on popcorn and a drink. You sit through all the previews, and finally the movie starts. Thirty minutes in, you realize you're bored. Maybe you don't care about the characters, or you find the plot unbelievable. Whatever the reason, the point is that you are not enjoying the movie.

Do you walk out?

Logically, you probably know you should. After all, how many times have you really disliked a movie after thirty minutes but ended up really happy about watching the whole thing? Let's say that happens around one time out of ten—so there's only a 10 percent chance you're going to end up liking this movie. Those aren't very good odds, but the sunk cost fallacy can trick you into staying to find out.

"I've already spent $25," you think. "Might as well get my money's worth." Or maybe you think, "I'll give it another fifteen minutes. Maybe it will get better." Then fifteen minutes pass, and it's still not good, but now you've sunk forty-five minutes into the movie. "I'm practically halfway through," you think now. "Might as well finish."

If you pay $25 for a movie, that money is gone, whether you like the movie or not and whether you stay for the whole thing or not. The choice you're now making is whether you're going to enjoy the next hour and a half of your time. You can either leave after thirty minutes and go do something you actually enjoy, or you can stay and—most likely—spend a full two hours bored.

With only a 10 percent chance you'll end up liking the movie, leaving is clearly the better choice, the one more likely to maximize your potential happiness. But the $25 you spent, along with the sunk cost fallacy, distorts your thinking. You're more likely to stay because of the value you think you'll lose by leaving. You stay even though the money is gone either way, and you're more likely to get more happiness out of your time if you leave.

HOW TO COUNTERACT IT

As the old adage goes, "If you find yourself in a hole, stop digging!" I know—that's sometimes easier said than done. So here are some tips to help you put down the shovel and start making better use of your time, energy, and resources.

Focus on Future Value, Not Past Cost

A key feature of counteracting the sunk cost fallacy is accepting that *you can't change the past.* Any time, effort, or nonrefundable money already given to the task is gone. It is irrelevant to the decision to continue or not. All that matters is looking forward.

This logic is, in principle, easy to apply to projects, at home, or at work. Say you're working with a group on a sales pitch and it becomes clear that the customer has new requirements that are totally at odds with how you're currently planning on pitching your product. Should you double down on the current project just because you've already spent a lot of effort on it? No. Your prior effort is wasted either way, and looking forward, the pitch has almost no chance of succeeding. There's no point throwing additional resources at a project that won't meet your customer's needs.

To decrease the effect of the sunk cost fallacy, separate yourself emotionally from the investment you've already made. Approach the decision as if you're a stranger learning about this project for the first time. Looking at where the project is right now and where it's likely to go from here, would you want to jump on board? What amount of effort and resources would you be willing to invest in it? Whatever your answers, they should significantly inform your decision to continue with the project or not. If you're having trouble emotionally separating yourself from the situation, try consulting a neutral third party.

The past is the same either way, so don't base your decisions on trying to justify what has happened. Instead, your decisions should be based on improving your outcome in the future.

Build an "I'm a Learner" Identity Instead of an "I'm Right" Identity

If you've dedicated significant time, money, or energy to something, you must have thought it was a good idea at some point. If you later decide to abandon the project, movie, relationship, or whatever else, that can mean admitting you were wrong, which can sting, especially if you identify as someone who is usually right.

This goes back to fixed versus growth mindsets. Instead of identifying as someone who is right, try to identify as someone who learns and improves. If your identity is tied up in being right, you will cling to your past decisions and keep digging yourself into a hole in your attempt to prove your past self right. On the other hand, if you identify as a learner, you'll focus instead on all the new information you've gained along the way. Instead of trying to prove the rightness of your past self, you'll be focused on how you can take what you've learned to do better in the future and build a better version of your future self.

The sunk cost fallacy makes you think that whatever you've already invested is a complete loss if you change course, but this is rarely the case. You will have learned something from the experience—you'll have gained new knowledge or skills or grown in some way. So whatever time, money, or resources you've spent aren't wasted; they've bought you something valuable: lessons and growth.

THE STATUS QUO BIAS (OR DEFAULT BIAS): WHY WE STICK TO WHAT WE KNOW

Another major cognitive bias that can keep you stuck in the same place or headed down the wrong path is the status quo bias, also called the default bias.

Do you use the internet browser that came preinstalled on your phone, or have you switched to one you installed yourself?

If you went to college, did you take the standard track of classes to fulfill the "core requirements," or did you design your own track?

Are you registered as an organ donor?

The most common answers to all of these questions, and many others that probably matter even more for your job, your relationships and your happiness, are strongly influenced by the default bias.

WHAT IT IS, AND WHY WE DO IT

The status quo bias is our tendency to stick to the default. It's a type of behavioral inertia. You've heard Newton's first law of motion: an object at rest stays at rest and an object in motion stays in motion unless acted upon by some force. In our case, behavioral inertia means we all tend to continue to behave as we have in the past and to prefer things as they are rather than changing them.

When faced with a choice, we all have a surprisingly strong tendency to accept the default option presented to us, even when the effort or thought involved in changing to another option is trivial. As with the sunk cost fallacy, many studies show the power of this bias.[9]

One excellent example of the status quo bias in action is organ donor rates.[10] In many countries, either a very high percentage (over 85 percent) or very low percentage (under 25 percent) of people register as organ donors. The disparity has little to do with beliefs about organ donation and far more to do with how the choice of organ donation is presented. Organ donation registration is often linked to some other official process, such as registering to vote or applying for a driver's license. In that process, depending on the country, people are either asked to opt in to being an organ donor, or to opt out. In the first situation, the default is *not* being an organ donor, and action (checking or clicking a box) is required to become a donor. In the second, it's the reverse—you *will* be registered

---

9   See, for example, W. Samuelson and R. Zeckhauser, "Status Quo Bias in Decision Making," *Journal of Risk and Uncertainty* 1 (1988): 7–59, and D. Kahneman, J. L. Knetsch, and R. H. Thaler, "Anomalies: The Endowment Effect, Loss Aversion, and Status Quo Bias," *Journal of Economic Perspectives* 5, no. 1 (1991): 193–206.

10   E.J. Johnson and D.G. Goldstein, "Do Defaults Save Lives?," *Science* 302 (2003): 1338–39.

as an organ donor unless you actively check or click a box to take yourself off the list.

In either scenario, you have complete freedom to choose to become an organ donor or not, and the effort involved to express that freedom is minimal, arguably trivial—check one box to opt in or opt out. And yet the setting of the default option dramatically affects the outcome of the process. Those countries with very high rates of organ donors? Their default is for everyone to be an organ donor unless they opt out. And those countries with low rates of organ donors? The default is for everyone to *not* be an organ donor, unless they opt in. That's the power of the default, or status quo, bias. A different default option on the form makes the difference between organ donation rates under 25 percent versus over 85 percent.

Sometimes, as with the organ donor example, which web browser we use, or what stereo is in our car, there's a clear default choice presented to us. We usually don't think about the fact that the default affects our choice so strongly, but we understand and can recognize that there is a default selected. At many other times in our lives, the default is simply to do nothing—to continue down paths we are already on. The status quo bias tends to keep us on these paths not because we consciously think they are still the best for us but because they are familiar to us. These paths may have been reinforced by prior decisions or habits; long-standing expectations from our family, friends, or peers; or our own assumptions or beliefs about such external expectations.

Why are we so predisposed to the default option? Our brains generally try to avoid both effort and uncertainty. Change involves both of these things. Remember that your brain evolved to keep you alive, not to make you happy. If you have a comfortable enough life, with adequate food and shelter, why would you waste valuable energy to make a change and risk losing that? In terms of survival, it seems better to stick with what you already know is working (at least well enough). Additionally, humans are social creatures. There were likely evolutionary benefits to fitting in and sticking to the status quo. For much of human history, if you were to be cast out by your tribe, you would be less likely to survive. So accepting the default option presented to you by a presumed authority—like the elders of the tribe—probably made sense.

As with the sunk cost fallacy, our tendency toward the status quo does have a purpose. Just imagine how time-consuming and exhausting it would be if you meticulously weighed your options for every trivial decision instead of occasionally accepting the default. Knowing that, you also need to be aware of when this bias leads you down the wrong path.

HOW IT IMPACTS DECISION-MAKING

The problem with the status quo bias is that the default option is not always the *best* option for us or even necessarily a good one. As we grow and learn more about ourselves, which option is best for us is likely to change. But the status quo bias keeps us stuck in the past, restricting our growth and keeping us on paths meant for the people we used to be, rather than who we are or, more importantly, who we want to be in the future. Our behavioral inertia carries us forward on our current path, whether or not we actually want what lies ahead on this path.

One of the best examples I've seen of how the status quo bias affects major decision-making involves a colleague from residency—I'll call her Sophia. Sophia was, in many ways, exactly what residency programs are looking for. She was smart and hardworking. She had excelled in college and then in medical school, and she was on the expressway to general surgery success.

There was one issue: she hated surgery.

Her parents had always wanted her to be a doctor and "not just any doctor." Surgery fit the bill and had seemed interesting to her, so she launched herself down that path. Somewhere along the way, she realized she didn't want to be a doctor anymore. She wasn't sure she had ever really wanted it.

But she kept going. Part of this was the sunk cost fallacy, but there was more at play. Sophia was a good friend, and we talked in depth about her feelings and challenges many times. When we would talk about this, she didn't talk about the time or money she'd invested so far to become a doctor. She talked about how, her entire life, she'd always thought she would become a doctor. It was the default option to the extent that she couldn't remember if she had ever consciously chosen this path or simply come to accept it.

To say that general surgery residency in the United States is challenging is an understatement. The educational requirements are hard, the hours can be astonishingly long, and the emotional challenges are intense. Most who go through the experience are fundamentally changed by it. They look back on it as a formative time, but one they would never go through twice. Point being, there are far easier ways to make money, to help people, and to build a respectable career. Yes, Sophia had student loans she needed to pay back, but she was a bright, resourceful woman who could have easily found other, well-paying employment. She could have left the medical field, but she never did. The status quo bias was so strong in her that she'd rather tough out the grueling work of residency than change paths.

Today, Sophia is a surgeon. In that sense, her inertia helped her achieve a challenging goal. But was that the real goal she wanted to achieve, or was being a surgeon only a goal because she expected it to make her happy, or fulfilled, or content— none of which happened? Did her inertia serve her well?

The more we repeat certain patterns—the longer we have been moving in one direction down one path—the stronger the "default" nature of those behaviors. The stronger the pattern of default behavior, the easier it is to continue down that path without even thinking about it as a choice. Just like the sunk cost fallacy, the status quo bias is rooted in the *past*. It tricks us into following a path based on whatever we've done or decided in the past instead of following the path that will lead to the future we desire.

HOW TO COUNTERACT IT

Remember my earlier question about which internet browser you use? A study found that Firefox and Chrome users significantly outperform Internet Explorer and Safari users at work and stay in their jobs 15 percent longer. As psychologist Adam Grant explained, it's not about the browsers themselves; "it's about being the kind of person who takes the initiative to doubt the default and look for a better option."[11]

---

11   Adam Grant, "The Surprising Habits of Original Thinkers," TED2016, February 2016, https://www.ted.com/talks/adam_grant_the_surprising_habits_of_original_thinkers.

As this study shows, your ability to counteract the default bias could very well lead to greater success and happiness. So like author Tori Eldridge said, "Never become so attached to following the path that you cease to question whether you should still be on it."

⁓⁓⁓

To counteract the status quo bias, we must move beyond what is, and consider what could be.

⁓⁓⁓

I have another friend from residency—let's call him Jacob—who faced similar issues to Sophia. He hated the pressure and was paralyzed by fear of making a mistake and hurting someone. Eventually, Jacob left medicine altogether. His loans are paid off, and he supports his family with a fine, non-medical job. He is never on call, and he doesn't have the stress of life-or-death decisions or the threat of getting sued for making any mistake.

When he left, there was the inevitable commentary in the halls, with people whispering that he "couldn't take it" and calling him "weak" and even a "coward." But you know what? Jacob is happy now. In overcoming his own inertia, he made the difficult, brave, and ultimately, I think, the better choice.

Though we're predisposed to the status quo, it *is* possible to counteract the default bias. The first and biggest step to counteracting it is, as always, being aware that it is real and affects us. The following two strategies can also be helpful.

Eliminate the Default Option with Forced Choice

Not surprisingly, if we can eliminate the existence of a default option, we can eliminate the default bias. We do this with *forced choice*, in which we must make a decision.

For organ donation, an example of forced choice would be asking "Would you like to be listed as an organ donor?" and then requiring respondents to select either yes or no. There is no zero-effort default option, and it requires the same amount of effort to choose either yes or no.[12]

Forced choice works well for forms, surveys, and any controlled situation where the opportunity for a zero-effort default can be removed. In many areas of our lives, though, there is *always* a default option: continuing in the direction we are already going.

When facing big life decisions—career changes, relationship choices, and so on—you can still re-create a version of forced choice. First, admit that you do have a default. Recognize that your education, family expectations, personal plans, and other internalized advice, values, or beliefs make you predisposed to a certain status quo.

Then, knowing that you have a default, make a conscious effort to view wherever you go next as a true choice. For example, if you're currently in corporate sales and wondering whether you should become a programmer, don't think of it as "Should I switch to programming?" Instead, frame it as "Do I want to be a salesperson or a programmer?"

---

12 The results can still be affected to some degree by the order in which the answer choices are listed, because we're slightly predisposed to see the first listed answer as the default, but forcing a choice in this way significantly decreases the default bias.

Imagine that where you are on the path is not just a fork in the road, but a T. You have to turn one way or the other. If you mentally stand at that intersection and have to make a choice, which path is actually more appealing for its own sake, rather than the seeming ease of coasting along on your current path? Make an honest assessment.

Do a "Life Evaluation"

Part of what makes the status quo bias so powerful is that we often don't even realize that we are settling for the default. One way to prevent this on a large scale is to do a "life evaluation."

A life evaluation is a chance for you to take stock of your life and the paths you're currently on. Even if you're not making big plans and are only taking it "one step at a time," your last step moved you in some direction. The default is that your next step will keep moving you in that same direction. You may not feel deeply wedded to whatever path you're on, but you're heading somewhere. A life evaluation will help you see where.

Think about your career, your relationships, your hobbies, your family—everything that is important to you in life. Consider what the default is in each area, and think about the different options that are available to you. Then use your technique of forced choice. Consciously decide if your current direction is the one you want or not. Note the areas where you have significant doubts or where you are sure you want to chart a new path. (We'll talk about ways to sort through big and small areas of life re-prioritization later on, in Chapter 5.)

The point of this exercise isn't to change things just to change them. It's to make sure that where you're headed is where you want to go. Often, your life evaluation will end up reaffirming your current path, but it's still important to do the work. You won't know if the evaluation will prompt a change unless you actually do the evaluation. Also, even if you don't make a big change, by consciously choosing and turning toward your path instead of passively coasting onward by default, you will feel more motivated and grateful for your direction and your opportunities to pursue it.

I deliberately do a life evaluation at least once a year, and I recommend the same for you. You want to do it regularly, so you can get ahead of the status quo bias before it becomes too ingrained. Pick a special date to help you remember to do it again, like New Year's Day, your birthday, an anniversary, or so on, and put it on your calendar.

When it seems useful, you can also do the same exercise on a smaller scale. Work seeming dull? Maybe it's time to do an evaluation of your current job or career. Jealous of your friends who moved to Ecuador last year? Perhaps you should reevaluate whether to stay in your current city.

Again, you will hopefully find that, for most things, no major upheaval is necessary or desired. But if something nags at you, don't forget that it's still a choice, even if it's been a long time since you considered it one.

KEY TAKEAWAYS

- You have a strong bias to stick with the default option in any choice.
- Your behavioral inertia will tend to keep you moving in the same direction, whether or not it is actually the best path for you.
- To fight against the status quo bias:
  - Set up decisions as forced choices, or as close to it as you can get, with no default option. Turn one way or the other, but don't view any path as straight ahead from where you are now.
  - Do a "life evaluation," in which you take stock of where you are, where your inertia is taking you, and where you actually want to go.

EVERY CHOICE IS A BET

Making big decisions can be scary. If you're going to majorly change your life, you want to be certain that you're making the right decision. But here's the thing: *all decisions, including not deciding, are made in uncertainty.*

In the midst of the COVID-19 pandemic, a lot was written about how we'd been plunged into uncertainty. I write a question-and-answer advice column for a medical student publication, and during the pandemic, my head editor asked me to write "something about decision-making in times of uncertainty." At the time, I thought, *Well, I'm writing a whole book.* But I wrote the column as well, and I explained that COVID-19 did not *create* uncertainty; it simply *highlighted* it. Twelve months before COVID-19 broke out, the future was just as uncertain as it was smack in the middle of the pandemic. The only thing that had changed was our awareness of the uncertainty. The future is *always* uncertain. Unlikely things—like a pandemic, an earthquake, finding a winning lottery ticket, being struck by lightning, whatever—are always possibilities. When we're confronted with an unlikely event actually happening, the future simply *feels* more uncertain.

You can work on decreasing your uncertainty by gathering information and learning from others' experiences, but ultimately, you must acknowledge and accept that you cannot know for certain how any decision will turn out because you can't predict the future. You could buy a house and then a year later a neighbor from hell moves in next door, or you could take one job over another and end up meeting the person who becomes your best friend for life.

Faced with all this uncertainty, what are we supposed to do? Annie Duke, PhD candidate in cognitive psychology turned multiple-time World Series of Poker champion, advises "thinking in bets."[13]

We sometimes have a tendency to look at life and our decisions like a game of chess. In chess, both players can see all the pieces all the time. All the potential moves of each player are known to both players. There are no hidden pieces, no random events, no secret capabilities of pieces on the board. The players are limited by their ability to imagine a number of moves into the future, but not by an inability to know what pieces the other player has in play or what those pieces are capable of.

Life is not like chess. In life, there is information we know, information we don't know but understand is missing, and the infamous "unknown unknowns"—the things we don't even know we don't know. Life is more similar to poker, where we know what we've got, but we don't know what we might get next, and we also don't know what the other players have. We send them signals, and they send us signals,

13 This is also the title of her great book on this topic: Annie Duke, *Thinking in Bets: Making Smarter Decisions When You Don't Have All the Facts* (New York: Portfolio, 2018).

but we can only guess at what those signals mean. We must take all the information we have and make a bet, even in the face of all the uncertainties.

Making decisions works the same way. Every decision is a bet. The final outcome of your choice will be influenced by the quality of your decision, and also by some amount of influence outside your control—effectively, luck. You can't actually know with 100 percent certainty how any choice will turn out. When you make a choice, you are betting that the action you take is the most likely to result in the outcome you want (or to avoid an outcome you do not want).

~~~~~

You're responsible for the process, not the outcome. You can't control the future. All you can do is make the best decisions you can.

~~~~~

At first, acknowledging that your choice is a bet can be disheartening. Why put all this effort into making a good decision if you still won't know how it will turn out? If that's how you feel, first know that you're not alone. Then, realize that *not* making a decision is still a bet—you're simply betting on the default, which may not be the best bet. If you want things to go well in the long run, you want as many bets as possible to go your way. So put the effort into making the best bets you can.

IT'S NOT ALL OR NOTHING

Too often, we view decisions as absolute and set in stone. We think they are irreversible, or at least too costly (in money, time, or effort) to reverse. So we view them as strong commitments, and we feel an immense pressure to get each of them "right."

But here's a secret: there is no such thing as a perfect decision. No decision, no matter how great it turns out, is 100 percent "right." And the reverse is true as well. Even if you make the "wrong" decision, it's not going to be 100 percent wrong. You will gain valuable lessons and experience that may serve you well in similar situations or in completely unexpected ways later in life.

Take my own career, for instance. You could say I made "wrong" decisions by majoring in physics and going into engineering. After all, I didn't like being an engineer and ended up putting in a lot of work and time to switch to being a doctor. My engineering experience and physics background opened up later opportunities for me, though, like working with an AI startup doing global health work. I never could have predicted or planned for that unique opportunity, and I wouldn't have been at all suited for it if I hadn't had that uncommon combination of prior experiences.

Being an engineer also showed me what I *didn't* want, so that I could get more clear on what I *did* want. Sure, from a career standpoint, as a doctor I'm several years behind where I would be if I'd gone straight into medicine. But my life overall is much more interesting, fulfilling, and, I believe, better because I made those "wrong" choices and learned from those experiences.

Most decisions are also more reversible than you might expect, and the cost of changing is often less than you first imagine. If I had discovered that I disliked medicine, I could have gone back to engineering. If you move to a new state and end up regretting it, you can move back. There are costs that go with making a change after a big decision, but they are usually costs that can be more easily borne than our initial reactions make us think.

Remember: every path you set off on is an experiment, and every choice is a bet. So don't let yourself be paralyzed by indecision or tricked into settling for the default. Be aware of the sunk cost fallacy and the status quo bias, and watch out for how they tend to keep you moving in the same direction whether or not it is actually the best path for you. Focus on the future, not the past, and use forced choice to overcome your behavioral inertia.

All decisions come with opportunity costs, including "not making a decision." No matter what, you are making a choice, so you might as well make it a conscious one, just like my fourteen-year-old daughter with gymnastics.

We've established that it's better to make a conscious choice, but how can you make sure your choices are the best bets? The bad news is that even when we are conscious about our decisions, cognitive biases can still get in the way and cause us to make poor bets. The good news is that there are strategies you can use to counteract these biases, just like the sunk cost fallacy and the default bias. In the next chapter, we'll look at the biggest mistakes we tend to make in decision-making and how we can start to improve.

CHAPTER 3

——

WHY GOOD BRAINS MAKE BAD DECISIONS

Those who cannot change their minds cannot change anything.
—George Bernard Shaw

Not too long ago, I was in the market for a new car. I was looking for three things: reliability, comfort, and fuel efficiency. I headed out with my checklist in mind and quickly got sucked into comparisons. This car got two miles more per gallon. This one had heated leather seats. Yet another had a fancy navigation system. I took several out for test drives and ended up falling in love with one of them. It was comfortable and fun to drive. Plus, one of my favorite songs happened to come on the radio during the test drive, and it sounded great through the state-of-the-art speakers. The car was significantly more expensive than some of the others I'd looked at—by several thousand dollars—but it was worth it to me. I pulled the trigger and bought it. When I drove it home, I was thrilled. I had made a great decision, I thought.

A few months later, though, I hardly ever thought about the

car or those amazing features I thought would be so important. Why would I? How often do *you* think about your car?
I'm guessing you don't wake up every day and think, "I sure
love my car and can't wait to drive it." Or if you don't have
a car, how often do you think about, say, your microwave or
your TV or your chair? Even when driving, I wasn't thinking
about how cool my car was. I was thinking about my email
inbox, the patients I would see that day, or an argument I
had the night before. If someone asked me how I liked the
car, I would say, "It's awesome. You have to check out this
stereo!" But in my day-to-day life, the car didn't make me
any happier than my old car had, because 99.9 percent of
the time, I wasn't thinking about whether I had one car or
another. I was just thinking about getting from point A to
point B, if I was paying attention to the current moment at all.

What happened here? I had successfully avoided the trap of
not making a decision. Even though I was comfortable with
my old car and had poured a lot of money into it to repair
it, I didn't let myself fall into the status quo bias or the sunk
cost fallacy. I recognized it was time for a new car, then put
a lot of effort into making the right decision. I compared my
options, tried them out, then picked the very best one. I was
so happy with my choice when I made it. But only a short
time later, the happiness faded. I wasn't any happier than I
had been, despite spending several thousand dollars extra.

So had I really made the right decision? It wasn't the worst
choice I could have made, but it certainly wasn't the best
either. While I avoided some cognitive biases, I walked right
into other psychological tendencies that can derail decision-
making. Chances are, you too have experienced these same
biases. They affect our thinking in nearly every situation,

whether we are aware of them or not. These next biases we will discuss are the distinction bias, the peak–end rule, and hedonic adaptation. Often, our decisions are more affected by these biases than by the logic of the situation itself, so it's important to become aware of them and how to counteract them when needed.

DISTINCTION BIAS: ARE YOU FOCUSING ON THE WRONG THINGS?

Think about the last time you bought something on Amazon (or a similar retailer). Whether it was as small as a water bottle or as large as a grill, what was your shopping process like? Did you buy the first item you found that met your criteria? Or did you keep searching and searching, and comparing and comparing, looking for the "best" option? If you kept shopping, did you end up buying more than you set out for, based on small details or features that weren't important to you until you started comparing options? You may have been falling into the distinction bias.

WHAT IT IS, AND WHY WE DO IT

The distinction bias is part of our natural tendency to focus on the distinguishing characteristics—the differences—when we have to decide between two (or more) things. This is even more powerful when the things we are choosing between are almost completely the same. The more similar two options are, the more effort it takes to tease out, focus on, and understand the differences. Our brains have evolved to understand that if we are putting a lot of effort and focus on something, then it must be important. So, the more similar two items are, the harder it is to identify the differences between them, and the more our brains trick us into thinking those tiny differences are vitally important.

If you were an early human, the distinction bias could be helpful. Choosing the slightly better food to hunt or gather, the slightly better partner to mate with, or the slightly better place to make a home could give you a competitive advantage in terms of survival. Nowadays, though, for many of our choices, *all* the options are so good that getting a slightly better version doesn't really matter.

In simple terms, with the distinction bias, if you're given multiple options, you will identify the "best" one. This may be based on tiny and potentially meaningless differences, but once you've identified it as "best," that's the one you want. If you had been presented with any of the other, "worse" options individually, you would have been more than happy with them. But when they're presented in comparison, suddenly they don't seem so great.

HOW IT IMPACTS DECISION-MAKING

Research shows that the distinction bias can interfere with our ability to predict outcomes and thus screws up our decision-making.[14] The distinction bias effect is so strong that we often forget the similarities between the options.

---

14   C. K. Hsee and J. Zhang, "Distinction Bias: Misprediction and Mischoice Due to Joint Evaluation," *Journal of Personality and Social Psychology* 86, no. 5 (2004): 680–95.

Due to the distinction bias, we may not even notice that we are making our decision based on small, inconsequential differences that we focus on precisely because the options are nearly identical.

Let's say you're shopping for a new television. Modern television displays are astonishingly clear. The colors are fantastic, the resolutions mind- (and eye-) boggling. Even a midrange model outperforms what was top of the line only a few years ago. Any new TV you buy is likely to be a big step up. When you go to the store to look at televisions, all the models in the store are, fundamentally, nearly identical. Aside from differences in size, they all have the same base features—digital inputs, high-resolution and high-accuracy color displays, high-quality speakers.

And yet, when you stand in the store, you can see that there are differences. This model's black level is just a little bit blacker. This model has ultra-quad color correction. You don't know what that is, but you know the first model you looked at didn't have it. And that first model is starting to look a little bit small compared to these others…

What do we do in this situation? Usually we shop our way (or get sold) up the line. We buy a bigger TV, with more features than we came looking for, for more money than we needed to spend to get what we originally wanted. When we get home and put it in our living room, we like it a lot. A few weeks later, we still like it. But do we like it any more than we would if we bought the model we originally had in mind? It turns out, we probably don't.

In the store, it's easy to see those miniscule differences. But guess what: you're not going to have ten TVs hanging next to each other in your living room. (If you do, put me on the list for your next watch party.) Without that direct comparison, you're not going to notice that fraction of a percent difference in brightness of colors or darkness of blacks. The quality of your TV viewing experience will be more affected by the light from your windows, the comfort of your couch, the color of the wall behind the TV, and any number of outside factors that end up mattering more than the tiny differences you can detect when the TVs are side by side in the store. The distinction bias can make us waste a lot of time agonizing over slight differences without it resulting in any better outcome.

Another interesting aspect of the distinction bias is that it tends to be stronger with *quantitative* (measured, numeric) measures than *qualitative* (descriptive) ones. Because quantitative differences are easier to identify (one number will be bigger or smaller), they're often what we unconsciously focus on, even in situations where they aren't nearly as important as the qualitative differences—like big life, education, or career choices.

We're actually reasonably skilled at judging how qualitative differences between options will make us feel in the future, at least in comparison to the same judgments about quantitative differences. For instance, compare two jobs. The first job is boring, but there is a massage chair you can use in the employee lounge on your break. The second job is very interesting to you but lacks any such lounge perks. Gut instincts, careful consideration, and psychology research all agree on that one—you should take the more interesting job every time.

Let's say one difference is quantitative: salary. The first job pays $75,000 a year, while the second pays $65,000 a year. The vast majority of us have a gut instinct that says $75,000 would be quite a bit better, and when we consider it intellectually, it seems like a clear choice as well—an extra $10,000 each year is worth having a more boring job. But the psychology research says the salary difference is almost irrelevant in this case.[15] Why this is true is related to hedonic adaptation, which we'll talk about soon. Right now, the point is that the quantitative difference of salary is actually far outweighed by other, qualitative differences: the people we work with, where we can live, the commute, even whether or not we can see trees from our office window or not. But thanks to the distinction bias (as well as beliefs about money), the difference in salary *seems* more important. When we are comparing options side by side, it is easy to focus on the money—it requires little thought to compare two numbers. And we neglect the fact that (for most of us) the difference doesn't actually buy us much in the way of well-being.

If we directly compare items, we're always going to be able to find differences and identify a "better" option, but it is only better in the context of a side-by-side comparison. We forget that, once we make the decision, we won't be making a side-by-side comparison anymore. We'll just be living our day-to-day lives—and with nothing to directly compare to

---

15 Reference Biggie Smalls, "Mo Money Mo Problems." Or read: Andrew T. Jebb, Louis Tay, Ed Diener, and Shigehiro Oishi, "Happiness, Income Satiation and Turning Points around the World," *Nature Human Behavior* 2, no. 1 (2018): 33–38, https://doi.org/10.1038/s41562-017-0277-0.

and no reason to do so, those tiny differences don't matter anymore and may have even fooled us into neglecting more important, bigger considerations.

HOW TO COUNTERACT IT

Clearly, the distinction bias can be a big roadblock in effective decision-making, so let's talk about how to counteract it. As with all biases, awareness is a great first step, but for the best results, there are two practical strategies to use as well: (1) avoiding direct comparisons and (2) focusing on satisfaction instead of maximization.

Avoid Direct Comparisons

The distinction bias is only an issue in simultaneous, direct comparisons. So the easiest way to avoid the bias? Avoid direct comparisons.

This strategy goes counter to how many of us have been told to make decisions. We've been taught to focus on the details and carefully weigh the differences. For most decisions, though, you will be much better off *first* creating a checklist of what you want, in order of importance, and then looking at one option at a time, seeing how it compares to your list. By focusing on one option at a time, you're less likely to get distracted by the differences that are unrelated to your actual main concerns, especially the tiny differences that are only identifiable in a direct side-by-side comparison.

For instance, when I was buying my new car, instead of test-driving all the models the same day, I could've spread them out, looking at one car at a time so I was less tempted to compare them side-by-side. Of course, that approach is a little inconvenient and time-consuming, so it's not always feasible. At the very least, though, you can always make the mental distinction: you are not comparing option A to option B; you are comparing option A to your checklist and then you are comparing option B to your checklist.

Even looking at one option at a time, you may find yourself digging into tiny details. After all, you're still making a comparison: between your list and the option. If you find yourself focusing on something that's not on your list, take a step back and ask yourself, "Does this detail actually matter?" and "Where does this fit on my list of priorities?" Sometimes you'll discover something you hadn't thought of up front that you do want to take into account, and that's okay. If that's the case, add it to your list. But be honest—only put it on the list if you can find where it fits. Which of the things you originally listed is going to move down in importance to make room for this new consideration? By asking these questions, you can make sure you're not prioritizing something unimportant over your crucial checklist items.

Focus on Satisfaction, Not Maximization

In decision-making, some people are maximizers, and other people are satisficers. Maximizers will keep putting in effort to get the best possible option. Sound familiar to all you perfectionists out there? Meanwhile, for satisficers, once they find an option that meets their criteria, they choose it. They are aware that there may be even better options out there, but as long as they have an option that is good enough for them, they're not going to waste their energy, time, or money trying to find an even better option.

There's strong evidence that satisficing leads to greater happiness, faster decision-making, higher life satisfaction, less regret, better mental health, and lower anxiety and stress around decisions.[16] This makes sense. It's easier, faster, and less stressful to simply find an option you're satisfied with as opposed to finding the *best* option. There's only one best option, while there are likely multiple options you'd be satisfied with.

Right now, you might be thinking, "But that's settling!" Satisficing and settling are very different. When you settle, you're accepting something that is less than you want. With satisficing, you're getting everything you want; you're just not spending extra resources to get *more* than you want. You can set your standards as high as you want. But once your standards are met, there are diminishing returns for continuing to put in extra money or effort.

Say you're choosing a bottle of wine that is rated on a 100-point system. You could decide that you want one that is rated 97 or above. After ten minutes of searching, you find a $30 bottle that has 97 points. If you search for another hour or are willing to spend an extra $100, you might be able to find a bottle that has 99 points, but is it really worth it? The science says no—you'll actually be less happy having spent the extra time and money. Set your standards, then once you meet them, stop. Stop wasting more time, effort, or money on getting more than you need. Move on to the next thing that actually matters.

---

16   B. Schwartz, A. Ward, J. Monterosso, S. Lyubomirsky, K. White, and D. R. Lehman, "Maximizing versus Satisficing: Happiness Is a Matter of Choice," *Journal of Personality and Social Psychology* 83, no. 5 (2002): 1178–97, https://doi.org/10.1037/0022-3514.83.5.1178.

THE PEAK–END RULE: HOW MUCH CAN YOU TRUST YOUR MEMORY?

Have you ever gone on a long, strenuous hike with a big viewpoint? When you think back to that hike, what comes to mind? Do you remember the sweaty hours slogging up and down the trail, or do you remember that breathtaking view?

Or have you ever had a wonderful time out with your friends, but at the end of the night there was an argument, and you all went away frustrated and uncomfortable? When you think back on that evening, how do you remember it? Do you think of the whole evening as tainted and crappy because it ended poorly?

In both of these situations, the peak–end rule is at play.

WHAT IT IS, AND WHY WE DO IT

The peak–end rule is our tendency to remember and judge experiences based on how they felt at the peaks (the highs and lows of the experience) and at the end.

Some of the most interesting studies into this bias have to do with how we remember pain. In one such study, participants were asked to submerge their hands in very cold water (cold enough to be quite painful but not so cold as to be danger-ous or cause tissue damage).[17] There were two stages to the experiment—stage A and stage B—with some participants completing first stage A and then stage B, and some doing the reverse. In stage A, participants submerged their hands for sixty seconds while repeatedly rating their pain. In stage B, participants submerged their hands for a total of ninety seconds, also repeatedly rating their pain. For the first sixty seconds of stage B, the temperature remained the same as in stage A. For the last thirty seconds, though, the water temperature very slowly rose by a couple of degrees. At the conclusion of the ninety seconds, the water was still cold enough to be quite painful, but not quite as painful as it had been for the first minute.

When asked to compare the two experiences, regardless of the order they completed the stages, participants rated the longer version as less painful. In fact, when asked to repeat the experiment one more time and given the option of the shorter or longer submersion, the majority of participants chose the longer version. Yet the pain logs show that in both stage A and stage B, the pain was equally as bad for the first sixty seconds. So in choosing the longer version, they were signing up for all the same pain of the short version, plus an additional thirty seconds (50 percent longer!) of added suffer-ing. They chose to repeat the experience that had caused them significantly more pain! Why? The peak–end rule. Because the longer version was less painful at the end, participants'

17   D. Kahneman, B. Fredrickson, D. Schreiber, and D. Redelmeier, "When More Pain Is Preferred to Less: Adding a Better End," *Psychological Science* 4, no. 6 (1993): 401–405.

memories misled them into thinking the longer version had been less painful overall.

A study done with colonoscopies found similar results.[18] In a colonoscopy, a flexible camera is inserted into the patient's rectum, then steered all the way up through their colon. To put it mildly, people generally don't like this procedure. It is uncomfortable and can be painful at some points. In this study, for half of the patients, the colonoscopy was performed in the totally normal fashion. For the other half of the patients, at the end of the procedure, right before telling the patient the procedure was complete and withdrawing the camera the final few centimeters, the doctor let the camera rest for a brief period of time, without any pressure or twisting, allowing for a brief period of minimal or no discomfort.

When the researchers compared the pain logs for the actual procedures, the groups were, on average, the same. Yet when asked to think back on the procedure, those in the second group rated the experience as much more tolerable. In fact, when asked to describe the peaks and valleys of the procedure from memory, they described the entire procedure as significantly less painful than they themselves rated it during the experience.

These two examples focus on the "end" part of the peak–end rule, but studies have also shown similar effects based on peak experiences.[19] So, why are our memories so goofy? Storage

18 Donald A. Redelmeier, Joel Katz, and Daniel Kahneman, "Memories of Colonoscopy: A Randomized Trial," *Pain* 104, no. 1-2 (2003): 187–94.

19 B. L. Fredrickson and D. Kahneman, "Duration Neglect in Retrospective Evaluations of Affective Episodes," *Journal of Personality and Social Psychology* 65, no. 1 (1993): 45–55, https://doi.org/10.1037//0022-3514.65.1.45.

space. Our memory has limits, so our brains don't store entire large experiences.

~~~~~

Our memories only store a few key moments—a highlight reel of the highest highs and lowest lows (the "peaks") and the final impression (the "end").

~~~~~

It would actually be pretty inconvenient if our brains stored *everything*. If we wanted to remember how we liked a movie, for instance, it would take the full length of the movie to go through our memory of it. So instead, a fine dinner out with a sad ending is remembered as a sad dinner out. A hike that was mostly boring is remembered as jaw-droppingly beautiful. A colonoscopy where the doctor left the camera in our bum totally uselessly for some extra time is remembered as significantly less painful than the exact same colonoscopy without the extra camera-pointlessly-sitting-in-bum time. And instead of enduring just sixty seconds of pain, we choose to endure ninety seconds of more total pain just because it is a little milder at the end.

Peak-End Effects

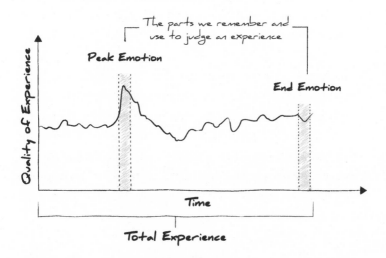

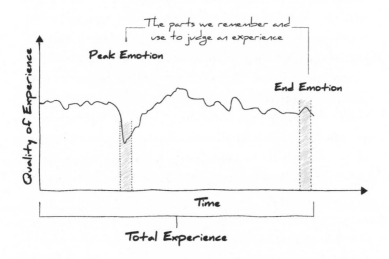

How It Impacts Decision-Making

Because we often rely on our memories of past experiences when making decisions, peak–end effects can wreak havoc on our decision-making.

As an example, I have a collection of fantastic memories about a road trip I took with a friend many years ago. We toured a couple of national parks. We saw bison and beautiful scenery. We stayed in a picturesque town and walked to the local bakery for a delicious breakfast. It was a wonderful trip. At least, that's how I remember it. If I were to decide whether to go on another trip like this one, based on my memories, I'd say yes, absolutely!

Interestingly, we can check the accuracy of those memories, though, as I kept a travel journal. And boy, does that journal paint a different picture! While plenty of people enjoy the travel aspect of road trips, I generally don't. And the trip was hot and mostly boring. There were a lot of long days in the car without much to see. Then we'd get to a destination and have half a day of pretty cool experiences, checking out the sights or the local scene. But for a two-week trip, those moments were few and far between. I only remember the trip fondly because of peak–end effects—I remember the highlights, not the day-to-day reality of the trip. If my goal is to maximize my happiness, I'm probably better off choosing a different kind of vacation.

If you are trying to make choices about your future based on your past experiences, it's important for you to have a handle on what those past experiences were really like. It would be a shame to never go on a boat again just because, on your first sailing trip, the captain said something rude as you were leaving. Or to buy a car because your favorite song came on the radio during the test drive and rocking out to it was the highlight of your day. Or to leave a career that is fulfilling most of the time just because of a few bad experiences with one coworker.

It makes sense to make decisions based on our past experiences, but when our memories of those experiences are inaccurate due to the peak–end rule, we set ourselves up for some big mistakes.

How to Counteract It

Fighting back against the peak–end rule is simple in concept, but not always easy. Your memories seem real to you. Your brain does not put up a red flag to warn you that it is reconstructing this particular memory from a few moments in the highlight reel. So it takes effort to counteract this bias. Though your memories may feel accurate and complete, remind yourself when making choices that all is not as it seems. Use these two tips to help get to the truth of your memories.

Go Beyond Emotion

Thinking about different choices will bring up emotions—happiness, fear, uncertainty, excitement. Our emotions are important, and we should be aware of them. But we shouldn't make our decisions based on emotions alone. Emotions are formed from our memories, and since we know we can't trust our memories completely, neither can we trust our emotions completely.

You have to consciously go beyond the emotions. If you're thinking about going back to school to get a chemistry degree, go beyond "Thinking about that plan makes me happy." That may simply be an emotion reconstructed from the fact that you always enjoyed the attention-grabbing, hands-on experiments, even though that was a very small part of chemistry class. If you're thinking about whether to accept an invitation to give a speech, go beyond "Ugh, I don't want to do that." You might only feel that way because your last speech went poorly, even if the ten speeches before that were great.

If you're going to use your prior experiences to inform your decisions (and you are, whether you're conscious of it or not), you should take the time to really reconsider those past experiences from a logical—in addition to the emotional—perspective. Think about them in pieces. Rather than thinking "I enjoyed that road trip," consciously break it down. What did you do each day? How was most of your time spent? Did you enjoy the bulk of your time? Try to simulate the whole experience in your head.

You can't actually be accurate in all this remembering—some of the information just isn't in your brain. Your brain will fill in some details, and you won't know what was real or made up on the spot by your brain. But the more you consciously break it down, the closer to accuracy you'll get. The more accurate memories you have, the more accurate predictions you'll be able to make about how you will feel in the future if you repeat an experience or make a certain decision.

Keep a Journal

If you want to know what *actually* happened, instead of just what you *remember* happening, a journal is a great idea. A journal is a place for you to record your experiences closer to the moment, less colored by the passage of time.

The usefulness of your journal in counteracting peak–end

effects depends entirely on the accuracy of your entries. A journal could easily become a microcosm of the peak–end rule if the only things you write about are the peaks, whether high or low, and your final impressions of various experiences. If you want this to be helpful in decision-making in the future, strive to be factual and to include information about the entirety of the experience. The more frequently you journal, the easier this will be. If you journal every day, for instance, it's easy to remember a lot of details. If you only journal once a month or during high-emotion times, the things you think to include will most likely be peaks or end experiences.

When it comes time to make a decision related to experiences you've had before, you can flip back through your journal to get a clearer picture of the reality of those experiences. This can be helpful for things that play out over extended periods of time, like travel, or even longer, like job and career choices, choices about where to live, or relationship decisions. Having a record of how things actually happened, rather than just your memory of the peaks and valleys, can help you make better informed decisions in the future.

KEY TAKEAWAYS

- Your brain stores highlight reels, not full events. Your memory is largely composed of the peaks (the highs and lows) of an experience and its last moments.
- Because your memory isn't an accurate representation of the full experience, you may incorrectly predict how future decisions will turn out.
- To counteract the peak–end rule:
  - Make a conscious effort to move past your emotions—think through your entire past experience, not just the highlight reel.
  - Consider keeping a journal so that you can double-check your memories.

HEDONIC ADAPTATION: WILL YOU LIKE IT NEXT MONTH?

Think of something you own that is important to you. A piece of jewelry, some exercise equipment, your cellphone, whatever. Now think of how you felt the moment you got it. The excitement of the thing, its shiny newness, playing with the features, wearing or using it for the first time. Now think of the *last* time you felt that excited about it.

If you're being honest, it's a good bet that item has never again made you as happy as it did when you first got it. For a while, you were probably still pretty excited about it. Every once in a while, out of the blue, you would think, "I'm glad I have this" or "Look how nice this is." But with time, the item faded into the background, and now, it probably doesn't enter your mind much. When you deliberately think about how nice your phone (or whatever) is, it might make you a little happy, but not as much as it used to, and you don't think about it that way very often.

That is hedonic adaptation in action.

WHAT IT IS, AND WHY WE DO IT

Hedonic adaptation is our tendency to revert to a baseline level of physical and emotional comfort. Essentially, we get used to whatever we consider "normal," and we don't get as much pleasure—or pain, depending on the circumstances— out of the same stuff or activities.

If my normal baseline happiness is a 6 out of 10, and I get a new computer that I'm super excited about, my happiness might go to a 9. But pretty soon, I'll drift back down toward

6, even though I still have the computer. It's not novel anymore, so it doesn't bring me much, if any, pleasure.

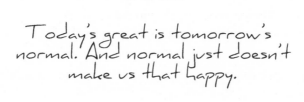

Today's great is tomorrow's normal. And normal just doesn't make us that happy.

Hedonic Adaptation

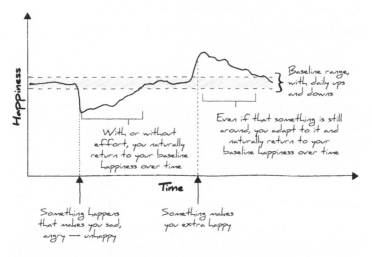

Plenty of studies demonstrate hedonic adaptation,[20] but this bias is one we're all personally familiar with. I'm sure you can think of quite a few examples in your life of things that were very exciting and increased your moment-to-moment happiness when they were new but don't bring you as much

---

20 See S. Frederick and C. Loewenstein, "Hedonic Adaptation," in *Well-Being: The Foundations of Hedonic Psychology*, edited by D. Kahneman, E. Diener, and S. Norbert, 302–29 (New York: Russell Sage Foundation, 1999).

happiness anymore, even though there's nothing wrong with them. That's exactly what happened to me with my new car. I was so excited about it, but then it became normal. We like to think we're special—the exception to the rule—but this is ingrained in our biology. The simple fact is that we like *new* stuff more than we like *nice* stuff.

As with all the other biases, hedonic adaptation exists for a reason. If we're never satisfied, if we always revert back to baseline happiness, we will keep pushing for something better. From an evolutionary perspective, you can see how that would be useful. In part because of hedonic adaptation, early humans kept looking for new and better ways to hunt, make shelters, and grow food, helping them to survive.

Even though it can push us to innovate, hedonic adaptation can also undermine our ability to be content or happy. No matter how much we have and get, we want more. It's important for us to be aware of this tendency and seek a balance between striving for more and appreciating what we have.

HOW IT IMPACTS DECISION-MAKING

Not accounting for hedonic adaptation can push us to make bad decisions. We tend to overestimate how happy a new thing, activity, or life change will make us in the big picture. We assume that if we're excited about it now, it will continue to make us happy in the long term. So we go for stuff that's new for the sake of newness. Along the way, we pass up options that are less shiny and exciting in the moment, but that would actually be much better in the long run.

Let's talk about money again, because hedonic adaptation

plays a role in the importance we place on it. We all know that money can't buy happiness, right? Well, sort of. It depends on how much money you already have. Studies show that increasing income and wealth does increase happiness, on average, but not in the same way for everyone.[21] The effect is sizable at extremely low-income levels, drops to a moderate effect for people at the poverty line, and becomes quite small by what most people in the United States would consider "middle income."

This makes sense. If you struggle to make rent and pay for groceries, money matters a lot. A surprise bonus of $500 would go a long way in that situation. But if you easily make your mortgage payment, your car is paid off, and you can afford to eat out a few times a month and travel now and then, a surprise bonus of $500 would be fun to get, for sure. But it wouldn't make much difference in the big picture of your life. And what if you owned several oil fields, a majority share in a large finance company, and several homes around the world? You'd probably be paying someone else to cash the $500 check and wouldn't notice whether they did or not.

Despite knowing that money doesn't buy happiness in most situations, we tend to overemphasize its importance. Let's return to the example of choosing between a job that pays $65,000 a year versus one that pays $75,000 a year. The extra $10,000 a year would seem amazing at first, but with time, it would leave your day-to-day thinking. You would rapidly adapt to your salary as "normal," and it would no longer bring you as much pleasure as it did. Five years down the line, you'll have made an extra $50,000, but the money

21   Jebb, Tay, Diener, and Oishi, "Happiness, Income Satiation and Turning Points."

won't make you significantly happier than if you'd taken the other job.

Again and again, we make decisions that we think will make us happy, but failing to account for hedonic adaptation leaves us with short-term highs but lacking long-term satisfaction.

HOW TO COUNTERACT IT

Hedonic adaptation can be challenging because it affects our current happiness as well as our choices about our future happiness. Thankfully, we can fight both the decision error and the adaptation itself, with some practice.

Practice Gratitude

We can offset some of the effects of hedonic adaptation with simple daily habits—namely, gratitude practices. Reminding ourselves about the greatness of what we already have can increase our happiness and well-being.

The best studied way to practice gratitude is also one of the simplest: write down three to five things each day that you are grateful for.[22] This doesn't have to be a long journaling exercise. Keep it short and simple, but be specific. List everyday items, people and their actions, and activities you are grateful for. This will improve your happiness and well-being within a couple of weeks and will continue to do so for as long as you maintain the habit. Gratitude meditations have also been

---

22 R. A. Emmons and M. E. McCullough, "Counting Blessings versus Burdens: An Experimental Investigation of Gratitude and Subjective Well-Being in Daily Life," *Journal of Personality and Social Psychology* 84 (2003): 377–89.

found to have similar effects, but there seems to be something about the act of writing by hand that increases the impact.

My experience with a gratitude practice fits the research. Some people like to do it first thing in the morning. Personally, I like to do it at the end of the day, as it makes me feel lighter and happier as I head to bed. I have also found that when I am consistent with the exercise, gratitude flows into the rest of my day. I pay more attention to little things that I'm happy to have. It's like my brain is prepping for a homework assignment, logging gratitudes during the day so that I can write them down later. That means that all through the day, I'm a little more aware of all the things I have to be grateful for, big and small: my family, coffee, a warm shower, my phone, someone holding a door for me, clean water, time with a friend, my health, my home, the grocery clerk checking my carton of eggs for breakage, my pets, and on and on.

You've probably already heard that gratitude is important. I really can't stress it enough. So much science supports the practice of gratitude.[23] But it only works if you do it. Commit to a daily gratitude practice for one month. It only takes five minutes a day. (For help with this, check out Chapter 9 on building habits.) Start small, and see where it gets you in the future.

Become a Time-Traveler

Being grateful for what we already have is great, but it doesn't help us make decisions about our future in any practical way. So how do we make decisions that serve us well even after

---

23   See, for instance, S. Allen, *The Science of Gratitude*, Greater Good Science Center at UC Berkeley, May 2018, https://ggsc.berkeley.edu/images/uploads/GGSC-JTF_White_Paper-Gratitude-FINAL.pdf.

we adapt to our new normals? Become a time-traveler. Not literally of course, though that would probably be helpful too. Figuratively, every time you make a decision, jump forward to the future. Instead of thinking about how happy the decision will make you right now, think about how you'll feel a few months, a year, five years from now.

If you're deciding between opportunities or activities—like choosing a job or hobby—consider if you will still be engaged over time. Does what you're considering offer new challenges and opportunities to be creative, not just in learning the new activity but as an inherent part of it? Note that creativity is not limited to "doing art." Creativity is the ability to create something new. Art counts, but so does creating a new engineering process, a more efficient way to get the rooms turned over between guests at an inn, a solution to a design challenge, or a new fundraising campaign for your organization.

You're more likely to still enjoy a job or activity several years down the line if it's something that gives you room to grow and experience new things. It might all be new right now, but it won't always be that way. Eventually it will become your normal and you will adapt, so think ahead. Time-travel several years down the line and ask yourself, "Will I get bored with this, or will it keep providing enough newness to keep me engaged?"

Take Breaks during the Good, and Power through the Bad

This final tip is another one that is more of a happiness hack than a decision-making hack. If we enjoy something, we typically avoid taking breaks during it, but if we don't enjoy what we're doing, we're more likely to take breaks to "make it easier to bear." Good research suggests we'd be better off completely reversing this usual pattern.[24]

I'm guessing you prefer to watch things without commercials. Who likes ads interrupting their show? At least one study shows that even though people don't like commercials, their interruptions can make the overall viewing experience more enjoyable.[25] When you spend uninterrupted time doing an activity you enjoy—like bingeing your favorite TV show— hedonic adaptation sets in. You start to get less enjoyment out of the activity the longer you do it. If you interrupt the experience, like with commercials, you can prevent hedonic adaptation, and you will actually enjoy the activity more. This applies to lots of different things. Taking multiple small vacations each year can have a bigger impact on your well-being and mood than one long vacation. Playing an hour of video games here and there is more enjoyable than playing eight hours straight. If you have dessert as an occasional special treat, it will taste more delicious than if you eat an entire cake in one sitting (and you'll feel less sick afterward too). By taking breaks from pleasant experiences, you get more excited to return to them and appreciate them more.

The reverse is true for unpleasant experiences. We tend to break them up into chunks because we think the breaks make them less painful. When we do this, though, we're actually disrupting the hedonic adaptation process. If you power through, you'll begin to adapt and get used to the unpleasantness. In the end, it doesn't feel quite as bad.

---

24 L. D. Nelson and T. Meyvis, "Interrupted Consumption: Adaptation and the Disruption of Hedonic Experience," *Journal of Marketing Research* 45 (2008): 654–64.

25 L. D. Nelson, T. Meyvis, and J. Galak, "Enhancing the Television-Viewing Experience through Commercial Interruptions," *Journal of Consumer Research* 36, no. 2 (2009): 160.

For me, as a doctor, being on call is stressful. I never know when I'm going to be called in, so I have to be ready to drop everything. I inevitably get woken up in the middle of the night and lose sleep too. In the past, I would space out my days on call, thinking that would be better. Now, I bundle them together and do a full week on call at once. Yes, it does suck. But after I get over the initial adjustment period—usually two days into the seven-day stretch—it becomes the new normal for me. It's not my favorite normal, but I can handle it. My overall frustration and stress level drops from, say, 9 out of 10 on each individual call day to a 6 out of 10 for the long stretch. So instead of having seven really crappy days spread out over a month, I have seven only sort of crappy days all in a row. Overall, I'm less stressed on call and I spend less time during the month dreading my next call. I'm more happy, more often.

To make hedonic adaptation work for you, break up pleasant experiences to decrease your adaptation, and avoid breaks in unpleasant experiences so that you adapt more.

KEY TAKEAWAYS

- You adapt to new circumstances faster and more completely than you expect. Things that initially bring you a lot of happiness likely won't bring you as much happiness in the future.
- Hedonic adaptation pulls you back toward your baseline after both good and bad experiences, even when you think those experiences will have a much longer effect on your happiness.
- To increase your happiness and well-being over time:
  ○ Establish a daily gratitude practice, in which you write down three to five things you are grateful for.
  ○ Break up pleasant experiences and power through the unpleasant ones.
- To improve the outcomes of your choices:
  ○ Stay conscious of adaptation, and consider how you'll feel about the long-term, day-to-day reality of your decision, rather than being distracted by how you feel about the decision as you're making it.

YOUR BRAIN IS AMAZING, BUT NOT PERFECT

Our brains are brilliant, wonderful things. They're our body's most complex organ, with billions of nerve cells that work together so that we can think and feel and dream. What they can do is downright incredible. But they're not perfect. Our brains have limitations, so they've come up with tricks and shortcuts to function and make our lives easier. Unfortunately, in some situations, these shortcuts become biases that push us away from, rather than toward, our goals.

In important decision-making, the distinction bias, the peak-end rule, and hedonic adaptation can get in our way more than they help. Fortunately, our brains are so amazing that, through conscious thought and action, we can counteract these biases when needed.

It's never too late to start improving your decision-making, and remember that your decisions are almost never set in stone. You know that expensive new car I bought? I ended up realizing that I'd made a poor decision, and I sold it. I instead bought the cheapest car that met my checklist of requirements—reliable, comfortable, with decent gas mileage. Every once in a while I miss some of the fancy features, but 99.9 percent of the time, I don't think about my car at all, and I'm just as happy now as I was after owning the expensive car for a while. Also remember that all decisions have an opportunity cost. Now that I don't have an expensive monthly car payment, I can spend that money on things that will bring me more happiness and have a bigger impact on my life—like taking my daughters skiing or going to a nice dinner with my wife.

Now that you have a handle on some of the major biases we're up against, you know what traps to avoid in making decisions. That's great, but life isn't just about avoiding mistakes. It's about moving forward to the future you want. That starts with defining your priorities and goals.

CHAPTER 4

—

FIGURE OUT THE BIG STUFF

"Would you tell me, please, which way I ought to go from here?"

"That depends a good deal on where you want to get to," *said the Cat.*
　—Lewis Carroll, *Alice's Adventures in Wonderland*

I don't think I can keep doing this, I thought after putting in another eighty-hour week at the hospital.

I had changed careers into medicine so that I could be happier and more engaged. After two years taking premed courses and getting experience as an EMT, I'd put in four years at medical school, and now I was in my first year of residency as a surgery intern. Technically, I was a doctor, but this wasn't the life I'd envisioned.

I was seeing as many as twenty trauma patients a day, and I was drowning in paperwork and grunt work, which, while essential, didn't feel particularly rewarding. My days were emotionally and physically draining, and I was gradually falling further and further behind on sleep. I wasn't happier, and I was disengaging. I was too physically and emotionally exhausted to feel any reward in what I was doing. I still had over four years of surgery residency left, and all I could see was the next exhausting day in front of me. I was so focused on surviving that I didn't look up at the future I was trying to build.

I could switch to radiology, I thought. It would mean redoing my intern year, but I'd always found radiology interesting. It was essentially solving puzzles—looking at black-and-white images and drawing on clinical information to diagnose and treat injuries and diseases. And while radiology residencies are far from easy, they are less emotionally loaded than surgical training and generally don't require as much of a time commitment. The radiology interns were definitely getting a lot more sleep than me.

I told my wife I was thinking about quitting surgery and switching to radiology. She had good reason to say, "Yes, switch!" The past months had been hard on her too. I was gone all the time, and when I was home, I was tired and stressed. Frankly, I wasn't much fun to be around.

Instead of encouraging me to quit, though, she reminded me of my big-picture goal: doing work that was meaningful to me. "Is that a goal you still want to achieve?" she asked me. "If so, you should stick with surgery. We're talking about a few years of investment to make the next thirty years of your career better."

She was absolutely right. I'd already considered radiology when picking my residency but ultimately dismissed it for the same reasons I'd decided to leave engineering. I wasn't happy as an engineer because I didn't find my work fulfilling. While radiology is undoubtedly important, it wouldn't give me the same sense of impact as being a surgeon. I wanted to be in the operating room, where I could directly see the positive outcomes of my work.

If it weren't for my wonderfully supportive wife and the fact that I'd already taken the time to figure out the big stuff— what I wanted from my life—there's a good chance I would've switched to radiology. And that definitely would have been a mistake. I would've spent the next five years working toward something that I didn't really want and that, when I stopped to think about it in the long term, I already knew wouldn't make me happy.

But because I knew what I wanted and *why* I wanted it, I was able to see past my current exhaustion and persevere. Instead of exchanging my future happiness for greater present comfort, I made the sacrifices needed to build the life I wanted. This is the power of having clear goals.

In the next chapter, I'll guide you through practical exercises that will help you define your long-term goals, but first, let's start with the big picture: why these goals matter, what makes us happy, what makes us feel like a good person, and the importance of passion and purpose.

WHY DO WE NEED GOALS?

Happiness isn't easy. Sure, short-term happiness might be easy—it can be bought with an entertaining TV show, a tasty meal, a shiny new gadget. But long-term, fulfilling happiness? That's a lifetime pursuit, and it takes work.

In any long-term endeavor—and a lifetime pursuit is about as long-term as it gets for an individual—you need a clear goal, something to work toward. You could be constantly taking steps, but if those steps aren't organized in a particular direction, they won't lead anywhere. You'll zigzag, backtrack, and wander, and either end up lost or right back where you started.

Without a destination in mind, you may be constantly moving without actually going anywhere.

To make progress, you need direction, and that comes from the "big stuff." So what's the "big stuff"? It's all the things you want most out of life—your big hopes and dreams for your career, your relationships, your hobbies, and so on. Goals are important, but not all goals are created equal. Whether you're aware of it or not, you have a hierarchy of goals. If you've made the effort to define it, the big stuff is at the very top. Long-term, top-level goals can be broken down into smaller mid-level and low-level goals.

As an example of a small hierarchy, consider going on a date. You may have the goal to look good for your date. But that goal is really to serve a different (higher) goal: to make a good impression on your date. Serving that same higher-level goal, you may also have goals of choosing a movie your date will enjoy and a restaurant you both will be comfortable at. And for each of those goals, there will be even lower-level goals or tasks—seeing what's showing at the local theater, looking up movie and restaurant reviews, and so on. So you have tasks, under low-level goals, under one or more layers of mid-level goals. Now step back. Looking at your life, is making a good impression on this particular date one of your *main life goals?* Probably not. Making a good impression is in service of an even higher-level goal—a goal perhaps about long-term companionship, or love, or family.

As you start to think about it this way, you might begin to see that, when defining goals, it is important to start at the top and work your way down. Writing out a bunch of tasks won't get you very far if they aren't organized around specific goals. And achieving those lower-level goals isn't going to mean much if they're not in service of a higher-level goal. If you are clear on your top-level goal, it can also help you move on when you fail at some low-level goals or leave some tasks incomplete. There will be other paths to reach your top-level goal, so any specific task or lower-level goal doesn't necessarily matter much for its own sake.

Consider the date example—picking a restaurant that turned out to be a dud may be a failure of a low-level goal you set for yourself, but it's unlikely to derail the entire process of finding long-term companionship in your life. The caveat here is that you have to treat that low-level failure as what it is: low level. If you go about the rest of your date and your future interactions acting like a disappointing menu was on the scale of a lifetime failure, you're going to miss out on opportunities to move forward. The opportunity cost of focusing on the subpar meal is the energy and time you could use to have other conversations or enjoy other activities together.

Achieving true top-level goals typically requires years of persistence. By clearly defining them, you can better map out and organize the smaller goals and steps needed to reach your destination and also increase your resilience along the road.

Hierarchy of Goals

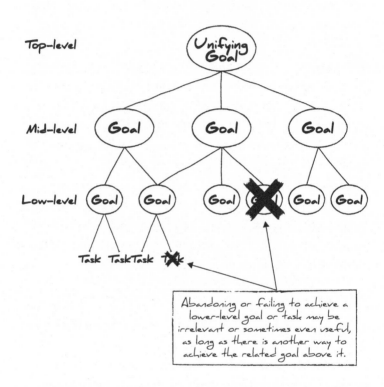

Abandoning or failing to achieve a lower-level goal or task may be irrelevant or sometimes even useful, as long as there is another way to achieve the related goal above it.

If you don't have all the big stuff figured out right now, don't worry. As J. R. R. Tolkien wrote, "Not all those who wander are lost." Wandering can serve a purpose. It can help us to better understand ourselves—our likes and dislikes, our talents, the things that bring us meaning. But there's a big difference between purposeful wandering and mindless wandering. The goal of wandering should be to figure out the big stuff. You don't want to spend your whole life wandering, because chances are, you're not going to accidentally stumble upon your ideal destination. (Note that I'm speaking figuratively here. For some people, happiness might mean exploring and discovering new things. They might spend their whole lives "wandering," but I'd argue it's not wandering the way I use it here, as they are purposefully following the path that creates happiness for them.)

By figuring out what you want in the big picture, and then taking the steps needed to create that, you have a much better chance of building the future you want.

THE FIVE FACTORS OF WELL-BEING: WHAT MAKES US HAPPY?

It would be easy to just say "My goal is to be happy." But that's too vague to be very helpful. First, happiness is a little different for everyone. So you've got to figure out what you mean by "be happy," and then you can go about figuring out what will get you there. Second, the simple fact of the matter is that while we all want to be happy, we can be bad at making the decisions that will lead to the most happiness.

Here's a thought exercise to prove it. Imagine you are walking down the street. You look down and see, partially covered by some old dry leaves, a twenty-dollar bill. There is no way to know who lost the money or to return it to anyone. That twenty dollars is now yours! What would you buy with this out-of-the-blue money to make yourself happy?

Pause and think about it for a moment.

Now, imagine a different scenario. Let's say there's an experiment going on. The researcher approaches various people and gives them twenty dollars. For half the group, the money is given on the condition that they have to spend it on something for themselves before the end of the day. For the other half of the group, they have to spend it on something for someone else within the same time frame. Which of the two groups do you think was happier at the end of the experiment?

If you said the people who spent the money on someone else, you're correct. When researchers actually ran this study, the people who had to spend the money on someone else were significantly happier about the twenty-dollar windfall than the people who had to spend it on themselves.[26] When you imagined what you would spend your found twenty dollars on, did you think about buying something for someone else, or for yourself? Don't beat yourself up over this. One of the major findings of this study and others like it is that we pretty much all do this as our default: think of ourselves first and expect that to make us happier. This is an effect that, if we're being honest, all of us have experienced in our lives.

~~~~~

Our desire for immediate gratification causes us to choose a short-term high over a longer-term benefit.

~~~~~

26   Elizabeth W. Dunn, Lara B. Aknin, and Michael I. Norton, "Prosocial Spending and Happiness: Using Money to Benefit Others Pays Off," *Current Directions in Psychological Science* 23, no. 1 (February 2014): 41–47.

So what will actually lead to lasting happiness? Thankfully, a lot of research has been done on happiness and well-being, in both the short and long term, and some consistent themes and patterns have emerged.

First, money isn't everything. It's just a tool. While we sometimes get caught up chasing more money, we don't really want the money—we want what the money can buy us. Money itself won't make us happy, but what it provides can. Also, as discussed in the previous chapter, as much as we enjoy *getting* material things, *having* them doesn't continue to make us as happy.

If money doesn't make us happy, what does? A fancy job title? Respect? Power? Not quite. According to the research, these five factors are what make us happy[27]:

- Social connection
- Health and activity
- Curiosity
- Learning
- Giving

These five factors are well-established as the things that make all humans happier and more well in the long run. To choose goals that give you the best chances of happiness and well-being, keep these categories in mind. There are any number of ways to accomplish these things, so you can still personalize your goals to your individual tastes. That said, you can quickly narrow a field of choices down by remembering you want to build relationships, be healthy and active, discover

---

27 J. Aked, N. Marks, C. Cordon, and S. Thompson, "Five Ways to Wellbeing," Centre for Wellbeing, New Economic Foundation, 2008, https://neweconomics.org/uploads/files/five-ways-to-wellbeing-1.pdf.

new things, learn more about what interests you, and give back to others.

But goals take work to achieve. Even if you know your goals will help lead to happiness and meaning, if you're not *excited* about those goals, it'll be hard to motivate yourself to do the needed work. So there's another important ingredient you need: passion.

HOW DO WE FIND OUR PASSION?

Did you ever have a project in school that you just didn't care about? It mattered for your grade, but the topic was so boring that you can barely even remember at this point what it was actually about? How did that go? Regardless of the grade,[28] how much did you actually learn, and how did you feel about the final product you presented or turned in?

Now compare that to a project you were interested in—a paper, art project, lab write-up, or independent study topic that you were really fired up about. Again, setting the grade aside, how much did you learn? What was the quality of the work you produced?

The difference between the two is passion. What you get out of your work and the quality you produce depend on how much you enjoy the work—your passion for it. If you're interested in something for its own sake, it is energizing to work on it. It is satisfying and rewarding, and this drives you to put in more time and be more focused during that time.

---

28 Grades are so heavily weighted by other biases and considerations that they're a really poor indicator of learning or quality of work produced.

That focus decreases distraction and increases both creativity and productivity.

Clearly, passion is important—so what do you do if you don't know what fires you up? How do you find your passion? Short answer: you don't.

~~~~~

Passion is not found. It is created.

~~~~~

"Finding" your passion implies that there is "a passion" out there already developed and waiting for you to get to it. As if you will know on the first try whether something is your passion, like being struck by lightning. Rarely is that the case. First of all, the first time you try something, you're probably not going to be great at it. Even if you have a growth mindset, it can be hard to feel passionate about something you're not good at yet. Second, a true passion is something that will sustain your interest and energy for years to come. Often, the things you feel passionate about right away end up flaming out in a relatively short period of time. Once the "honeymoon period" is over, you're just not that interested anymore. This is hedonic adaptation in action once more. Something may be fun and exciting when it's new, but eventually, it'll become your normal. If it's not still fun and exciting at that point, it's not your passion.

Instead, as Dr. Angela Duckworth, author of *Grit: The Power of Passion and Perseverance* (which I highly recommend), said in one interview, "A passion is developed more than it is discovered."[29] This doesn't mean that drudging, life-sucking work will magically turn into something you are passionate about if you just stick with it long enough. But if a certain kind of work has meaning to you, has some aspects you enjoy, and isn't sucking the life out of you, it could be your pre-passion work. If you identify the areas that are most interesting to you and work on skill development and personal growth in those areas, you will grow your passion.

It's a cycle: feelings of accomplishment and growth reinforce your enjoyment, which reinforces the activities that lead to accomplishment and growth. Over time, the accumulation of positive feelings, sustained growth, and focused interest become just the thing many others are still waiting to "discover": a real passion for your work. As you gain understanding and skill, you may also develop a broader perspective of how your work benefits others, which can lead to a sense of purpose.

The problem for many of us is how to sustain that effort and focus in the early days. If we're not struck out of the blue by great passion for a job, (a) how do we know if it will eventually become a passion and (b) how do we stick with it long enough to get to the point where it actually feels like a passion? The answer to both questions is related to purpose. You may already be aware that a passion can develop into purpose, but it works in reverse as well: purpose can lead you to a passion.

---

29   Dan Shawbel, "Angela Duckworth: 'A Passion Is Developed More Than It Is Discovered,'" *Forbes*, January 9, 2017, https://www.forbes.com/sites/danschawbel/2017/01/09/angela-duckworth-a-passion-is-developed-more-than-it-is-discovered/?sh=511885c3c0b4.

HOW DO WE FIND OUR PURPOSE?

It turns out that to sustain interest and engagement over time, it may be even more important that you feel your work has meaning than for it to excite you. Having a reason outside of yourself for why you do what you do is one of the strongest predictors of satisfaction, advancement, and longevity at a job. Plus, as already discussed, giving back to others is a key factor of happiness, and by addressing a need in the world, you can feel more "deeply good." So if you want to know whether something can transform into a passion and ensure you have the motivation to stick with it until it does, purpose is a great place to start.

Thankfully, this doesn't mean we all have to be solving global poverty or working toward world peace with every hour of our career. What it means is that, whatever we are doing, we should frame it in a way that ties our efforts to something meaningful outside ourselves. Remember: mindset matters. How we think affects how we feel and act.

As an example, on a tour of a NASA facility, John F. Kennedy stopped and introduced himself to a man carrying a broom down the hall. When JFK asked the man what he was doing, he replied, "Mr. President, I'm helping put a man on the moon." This story can seem a little trite—it's *too* good, like it was made up to make us all feel good about our jobs regardless of what we're doing. But it actually happened! JFK was well known for taking the time to meet and speak with anyone and everyone along the way on such visits. The exact details aren't certain—in some versions of the story, the man is using the broom, not carrying it, or he has a mop instead. But presidential archives and interviews indicate that such an interaction did in fact occur.

Not only is this story true, but there are many others like it, as well as research supporting the idea. In a study of job satisfaction, Morten T. Hansen and a team of researchers interviewed and observed people at all levels of different types of organizations, from workers in a factory to senior business leaders to lawyers to sales reps.[30] Across all levels of every organization, finding purpose in work was strongly associated with job satisfaction and was also a predictor of success, as measured by both advancement and evaluations from peers and managers. The study also found that, within the same role, there was a huge range in how much purpose people felt their job had. This suggests that purpose comes not from the work itself, but from each individual's *perception* of the work. For example, in related studies among hospital cleaning staff, those who framed their work as helping people heal were happier at their jobs, had a better sense of balance between work and the rest of their life, and had fewer symptoms of burnout or depression than those who described their work based on the tasks they did. These people were also more likely to be rated above average at their work by their peers and managers and were more likely to be recommended to other positions.[31]

A sense of purpose comes not from your work, but from how you think and feel about your work.

---

30 Morten T. Hansen, *Great at Work: The Hidden Habits of Top Performers* (New York: Simon & Schuster, 2018). See especially chapter 5, "P-Squared (Passion *and* Purpose)."

31 Hansen, *Great at Work*, 108.

This doesn't mean that everyone will suddenly enjoy how they spend their time at work or at school just by telling themselves it's for a bigger purpose. You have to actually *believe* it. As an engineer, I could mentally come up with a purpose for my work. I was in research and development making electron microscopes, and I would tell myself that by helping produce this tool, I was contributing to all sorts of scientific studies that were bettering humankind. Honestly, that very well could have been true, but I never knew exactly how the microscopes were used or if they led to any important discoveries. No matter what I told myself, I just didn't feel that my work had purpose for me, even though lots of other engineers feel their work is very meaningful.

If you're struggling to believe in the purpose of your work, start with baby steps. Similar to passion, purpose is created more than found. In his book *Great at Work*, Morten T. Hansen details the "purpose pyramid."[32] At the base of the pyramid is the belief that your work creates value without doing harm. From there, you can move up to the next level: crafting personal meaning in what you do—what *you* find valuable about your work. Finally, you can reach the apex of the pyramid: a social mission, in which you connect your work to the value it provides to the world or other people. By accessing the base level of the pyramid first, then working your way up, you can build a stronger and stronger sense of purpose over time.

If this approach doesn't work and you still can't find any reason you're doing your job besides making money, it's time to face facts: this work does not provide you with a sense of

32   Hansen, *Great at Work*, 105.

purpose. That doesn't make you a bad person or mean that the work has no purpose. It means that this particular work lacks a strong sense of purpose for *you*. And that's okay. It simply means the job isn't a good fit for you, and likely also means you won't be able to develop or sustain a passion for it. It's time to choose change. This was the case for me with engineering, which is why I switched to surgery.

Since passion and purpose are both created rather than found, a good goal is to find work that leverages both. Either can lead to the other, so start by cultivating whichever comes more naturally to you, then work to combine them.

MAKING GOALS DOESN'T NEED TO BE SCARY

Determining your long-term goals can feel overwhelming. Deciding what you want out of your *entire* life? That's a lot of pressure. What if you get it wrong? You could end up wasting your whole life!

Relax. Take a deep breath. There are no right or wrong answers when it comes to top-level goals. The only ways to really screw this up are (1) to not set goals at all and (2) to never reevaluate your goals.

You now know which factors have been scientifically linked to happiness:

- Social connection
- Health and activity
- Curiosity
- Learning
- Giving

You also know that passion and purpose are each important, and that both are created rather than found.

The next step is to set goals that will bring you closer to those things in your own life. And remember: your goals aren't set in stone. No fixed mindsets here. It's quite possible you will change your mind about your goals in the future, and there's nothing wrong with that. You're striving for growth and improvement, not perfection. When I had that crisis moment during residency, I could have realized, "Actually, this goal isn't something I want anymore." I could have chosen to switch to radiology or even leave medicine altogether. It wouldn't have meant that I made the "wrong" goal; it would've meant that I'd changed or learned more about myself, so I needed to adjust my goals. This is what my friend Jacob (mentioned in Chapter 2) did in leaving residency and building himself (and his family) a happier life with a better career fit.

There's a reason people who set goals are more likely to achieve them: we need goals to give us direction and keep us focused. By consciously setting goals, you can make sure you're less swayed by temporary circumstances or in-the-moment emotions. You can keep your eye on the prize.

I'm not going to pretend that setting goals is easy. It can take time and effort. Fortunately, there are a lot of great exercises that can help. In the next chapter, we'll go through a few that many people find helpful and even fun.

CHAPTER 5

DEFINE YOUR LIFE AND CAREER GOALS

Most of us should spend less time on most decisions, and we should spend a lot more time on a few key decisions.

—RAMIT SETHI

Imagine you're on a boat in the middle of the ocean, and you're lost. You know that, in theory, you should be able to navigate by the stars. That's great, but unless you know a method of actually doing that, you're in big trouble. Similarly, you can know that long-term goals are incredibly important, but if you don't know *how* to go about making them, you may as well be stuck in the middle of the ocean, with a map in the sky you can't read.

That's what this chapter is for. I will guide you through several different strategies and exercises that will give you not just the theoretical *why* of goals but the practical *how*. All of these strategies have been studied and found effective, and they're all things I've personally used for myself and with others. You can do the exercises in any order you like, but I've put the exercises in the order I think is most natural, allowing them to build on one another.

I do recommend focusing on just one exercise at a time. You get out what you put in, so don't rush. I also recommend completing *all* of the exercises. Even if one doesn't seem particularly helpful, give it a try. If you really do hate it, you never have to do it again.

Each time I work through these, the way I think about myself and my goals get more refined and feel more "right" with each exercise, until I converge on a small set of goals and ideas that I can move forward with.

Here's a quick breakdown of what's ahead:

- Involve Your Future Self—This exercise is one everyone should do, repeatedly, especially when making a big decision. If you have a hard time predicting which decisions will bring you the most happiness or you have a tendency to prioritize present comfort over future gain, try this one out.
- Identify Your Ikigai (Create a Purpose Venn Diagram)—If you've ever felt like your interests, your strengths, what you think is important, and what you do to make money aren't aligned, this is the exercise for you. It can help highlight unexpected overlaps and promote making new connections between these areas.
- Pick Five Things—If you find yourself pulled in many directions or you're uncertain how to prioritize your goals, this is a great exercise. It can help you narrow your focus, so you can get better results on the things that matter to you most.

- Ideal versus Current Time Comparison—If you feel like you don't have a good balance in how you spend your time, this exercise can help pinpoint where you're out of alignment.

INVOLVE YOUR FUTURE SELF

Every choice you make will have real effects and opportunity costs for yourself in the near and far future. Some of those effects may be trivial—will I be happier with the macchiato or the flat white? Some may be dramatic—will I live to see tomorrow if I drive myself home after this party? But it will be your future self who lives—or dies—with those effects.

The number of people who will be affected by your choices varies, but there is one person who is always on that list: Future You.

Oddly, we are not particularly nice to our future selves. There are many possible explanations for this, and they're still being investigated and sorted out. One factor is our tendency to choose immediate gratification over delayed gratification (this is due to a cognitive bias called *time discounting*, which will be discussed in more detail in Chapter 7). We make our decisions based on what will make us most happy now and leave our future selves to sort out how to be happy in the future. Have the extra glass of wine—who cares if Future You has a hangover? Skip the stretching—Future You can deal with the soreness and potential injury. Take home 2 percent more pay now and have 70 percent less saved for retirement later—that's Future You's problem.

Another factor is related to compassion. We are less compassionate toward people we don't know or identify with than with people close to us. For instance, we think of caring for the elderly as a good idea in theory, but most of us don't do much to help the elderly in practice. But let's say we get to know one particular elderly grandmother at an assisted living center. We learn about how she traveled the country as a dancer in her twenties, and she shares her lemon bar recipe with us—the one her husband always asked for on his birthday—and tells us surprisingly raunchy jokes that make us laugh. Now if we're asked to help, out comes the checkbook and the calendar for volunteering.

Interestingly, we tend to treat our future selves the way we would treat somebody we don't know or have never even been introduced to. We think helping our future selves is nice in concept, but we're not attached to the idea enough to actually make many sacrifices in the present. With this next simple, two-step exercise, you can combat this tendency and make long-term goals that will be good for Future You in addition to present you.

STEP #1: ENVISION YOURSELF IN THE FUTURE

Picture yourself in the future. How old you picture yourself will depend on the decision you're trying to make. If you're trying to decide which TV to buy, you might want to picture yourself just a few months or a year in the future. If you're trying to decide whether to go vegan, you might want to picture yourself five or ten years in the future. If you're trying to decide on a career, it might make more sense to picture yourself twenty years into the future. For most decisions, it's helpful to picture yourself at several different points in the future, which is also what you should do if you don't have a specific decision in mind.

For now, envision yourself at sixty-five. Create a detailed picture in your mind. Better yet, create an *actual* picture, using digital aging software, an app, or filters. People who interact with a digitally aged version of themselves, in a photo or, even more powerfully, in a virtual reality setting, even for five minutes, subsequently save more for retirement.[33] If you're digitally challenged, no worries—even being asked to sit quietly and visualize ourselves as an older person changes our eating and exercise decisions in the short term.

Taking the time to picture an older version of yourself helps you see Future You as a real person you can care about, not just a stranger. You might even consider printing out a digitally aged version of yourself and keeping it at your desk, on your fridge, or anywhere else you'll regularly see it, so that Future You becomes a close companion.

STEP #2: ASK "FUTURE YOU" QUESTIONS

Now, holding on to your mental image or looking at the digitally aged photo, ask Future You questions that will help you make your decision in the present. You can ask anything you think is useful, but here are good questions to start with:

---

33   H. E. Hershfield, D. G. Goldstein, W. F. Sharpe, J. Fox, L. Yeykelvis, L. L. Carstensen, and J. Bailenson, "Increasing Saving Behavior through Age-Progressed Renderings of the Future Self," *Journal of Marketing Research* 48 (2011): S23–27.

- What is important to you? Financial security? Health? Your home? The stuff you own? Family and friends?
- What are you happy you did or didn't do?
- What are you proudest of?
- What do you regret?

Write down any insights you gain. Then, related to whatever decision you're considering, pick one of the options. Imagine the choice as if it was in the past and ask Future You, "Are you happy you made that decision?" Cycle through each potential option and ask the same question again.

Don't delude yourself into thinking you now know how you'll feel decades into the future. We all change far too much over time to really predict that. The point of this exercise isn't to become a fortune-teller; it's to get you thinking more effectively about the decisions that will serve you best in the long-term, rather than just in the present moment.

IDENTIFY YOUR IKIGAI (CREATE A PURPOSE VENN DIAGRAM)

Ikigai is a Japanese word that translates roughly as "reason to live." Ikigai and purpose are often conflated, but they're not quite the same thing. They're both a reason for being, but "purpose" suggests a grand, lofty goal you can dedicate your entire life to, while ikigai can be found in the smaller, everyday realities of life. In the Japanese philosophy, ikigai is the thing that makes you want to get out of bed in the morning, and it can be anything—it could be the ninety-year-old woman who gets up to see her grandchildren, or the forty-year-old man who gets up to help launch a new product at work, or the twenty-year-old college student who gets up to spend time with friends. Part of practicing ikigai is practicing gratitude—learning to appreciate what you have in life and cultivating a positive mindset. You can also have more than one ikigai, and it can change over time.

The exercise I'm about to show you is not really an ikigai exercise. If you look online or in other works, you will often see it called ikigai, but it is actually a Westernized framework loosely based on the concept of ikigai. Most accurately, it should be called a purpose Venn diagram. I've chosen to use the ikigai terminology as well, because understanding the concept of ikigai will help you get the most out of this exercise. This is what the Venn diagram looks like:

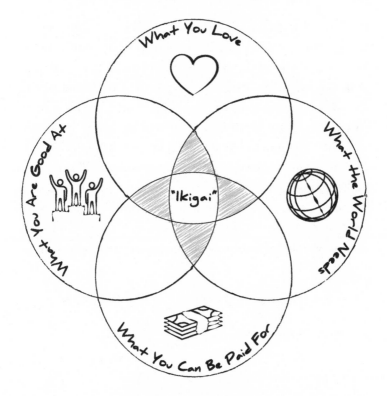

Like all techniques, this exercise is not magical. It is, however, very useful, especially in thinking through big life-direction decisions.

~~~

One way to get closer to your ikigai or purpose is to search for the intersection between things you love, things you are good at, things you can get paid for, and things the world needs.

~~~

I've done this exercise several times, and I have a tip before you get started: don't assume you know what your ikigai is. Sometimes when I do this exercise, I come up with things that surprise me on the margins, but usually I converge on the same items in the center. At this point, I'm beginning to wonder if my brain rigs the game, assuming it knows what is "supposed to" go in the center and thus building the options around the edges to create the "desired" outcome. Fight against that tendency. There's no point to the exercise if you work backward from what you think "should" be at the center for you. You have to work from the outside inward, and allow yourself to (maybe) be surprised by some new ideas.

ADDITIONAL RESOURCE: IKIGAI DIAGRAM

For a printable ikigai diagram, visit fredericbahnson.com.

STEP #1: PRINT (OR DRAW) YOUR DIAGRAM

Start by creating your diagram. You can print off a template from the internet, or you can draw your own.

STEP #2: LIST THINGS YOU LOVE

In one circle, list anything and everything you love and enjoy doing—for example, sailing, hiking, solving interesting problems, making things with your hands.

Some tips for success:

- Don't worry yet about whether you're good at these things, whether you could make money from them, or whether they're things the world needs. Right now the only thing that matters is whether you enjoy them.
- Make sure you are listing things you actually enjoy *doing*, not *having done*. For example, I think it would be really cool to be able to tell people I hiked to the South Pole. Would I enjoy actually doing that? Nope. Definitely not. It would be cold and exhausting and sounds utterly miserable to me. Avoid listing things you would like to be known for or that you'd like people to know you have accomplished. Focus on the things you enjoy inherently, for their own sake.
- Include both specific examples and broader categories. For instance, let's say you put sailing and hiking on your list. If what you love about those things is being active outside, you should put that on your list as well, as it will open up many more potential options.

STEP #3: LIST THINGS YOU ARE GOOD AT

In another circle, list the things you're good at—for example, practicing new skills, working with others to solve problems, sailing, making things with your hands. If you're using this exercise to set education or career goals, it makes sense to consider your strengths. You might love playing basketball, but if you're already an adult and still not very good at it, becoming a professional basketball player probably isn't your best career option.

Some tips for success:

- Again, focus only on your strengths right now. Don't worry about the other categories in the diagram.
- Include both specific and more general items, just like you did with the things you enjoy. When you list something specific, ask yourself, "Why am I good at this thing?" That could lead you to a broader strength you didn't realize you have. For example, maybe you're really good at jigsaw puzzles—that might mean you're good at pattern recognition, which is a skill that has lots of uses.
- Consider listing not only what you're good at right now but also what you think you could become good at. Remember that your skills and strengths are not fixed. If there's something you show potential in and you're interested in it or passionate about it enough to want to develop your skills, it's okay to include it here.

STEP #4: LIST THINGS YOU CAN GET PAID FOR

A fundamental aspect of well-being is having one's basic needs covered—food, shelter, and security—and that rarely happens without at least some amount of money coming in. So, assuming you're not already independently wealthy, what can you get paid for? List them in another circle—for example, handyman, building furniture, teaching.

Some tips for success:

- List only those things you could reasonably work your way into from where you're at now. The idea isn't to list every single possible job in the world. That would be a very long—and unhelpful—list. You need some boundaries on this. This is where leaving "professional basketball player" off the list is appropriate for most of us. It's definitely a thing some people get paid for, but not a thing most of us ever will get paid for, even if we try.
- Keep your mind open to the possibilities. This can be a tough balance. You need some boundaries here, but you don't want to get too aggressive, dismissing potential jobs as "unreasonable" or "off limits." A certain job might take a lot of time and work to be a possibility, but it's still a possibility. Leave off the truly unreasonable options, but challenging ones are okay.
- Again, be general and specific. You can list a particular role, like web developer, or an entire field, like computer science, or both.

STEP #5: LIST THINGS THE WORLD NEEDS

Now move on to the final circle, and list things the world needs—for example, access to education, safe shelter, and beauty.

Some tips for success:

- Focus on the needs you care about most. As with jobs, the world has a lot of needs. If you try to list everything, it'll be overwhelming. So instead, zero in on the needs you're passionate about, personally interested in, or think are most important.

- Think both big and small. The world needs people to address large issues like climate change, and it also needs people to address smaller needs, like the need for safe and secure homes or pets to keep us company.

Defining Your Ikigai

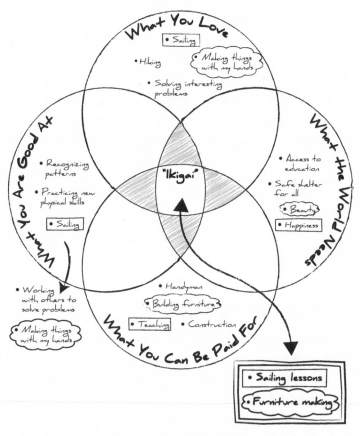

Other Ideas:
- Volunteer with Habitat for Humanity
- Teach vocational skills?
  - → Construction?
  - → Furniture-making?

STEP #6: DO A SECOND PASS, THEN LOOK FOR THE OVERLAPS

Go back and review each category a second time. Did things you thought of for later categories trigger ideas about things to include in earlier categories? Add those in now.

Then, look for the overlaps and add those into the diagram. For instance, in my example, there's an overlap between making things by hand (which appears both in "things you enjoy" and "things you are good at"), building furniture and being a handyman ("things you can get paid for"), and the need for both beauty and safe shelter ("things the world needs"). This suggests several different options you could put at the center of the diagram. Build furniture? Work in construction? Make inexpensive tiny homes? Join a nonprofit that works to house the homeless, either as a full-time job or as an intermittent volunteer?

The ultimate goal here is to try to find things that combine all four categories, but it's worth noting *any* overlap. Even if something only overlaps in two or three circles right now, you might realize that there's actually a way for it to check off every category. For instance, with the example I've used, sailing appears in both "things you enjoy" and "things you're good at." Looking at that overlap, you might realize, "Oh, I could totally make money through sailing! I could give lessons or take people on sunset sails. And hey, that actually solves a need in the world too—people need new experiences to be happy, and I'd be providing them an adventure."

What if you go through this whole exercise, and you don't find anything that overlaps in all four categories? First, go back, look at the specific things you've listed, and see if you can translate those into broad, general things. Do the opposite too, looking at the broad things you've listed and coming up with more specific examples within that category. Second, look at the places where you have some overlap and see if you can find ways to create additional overlap (as in the sailing example). After that, if you still don't have anything in the center of your diagram, don't worry! This is not an all-or-nothing exercise. Any overlap at all is a good thing. If you have overlap between what you love and what you're good at, that's a passion. Overlap between what you're good at and what you can get paid for is a profession. Overlap of what you can get paid for and what the world needs? Vocation. Overlap of what the world needs and what you love? Mission.

You can achieve ikigai without having an overlap in all four categories. In fact, not a single one of these categories is *required* for ikigai in its true form. Ikigai in the Japanese philosophy is about feeling that your life is worth living. You could experience ikigai doing a job you find meaningful but don't necessarily enjoy. You could experience it in taking your dogs for a walk on a sunny day. You could experience it volunteering at your kid's school. The point of this exercise is basically to identify the things that will get you the most bang for your buck. We all need things in our lives that we enjoy, that we're good at, that we can get paid for, and that help solve the world's needs. If we can identify one thing that does all of that, great! If not, that's okay too. You *are* allowed to do more than one thing—a revolutionary idea, right?

PICK FIVE THINGS

If you've completed the ikigai exercise, you likely have a lot of options to consider. Hopefully, many of those things overlap, or you can see how they might fit together in your life. But for the vast majority of people, they won't all match up. Some goals and activities will be completely incompatible with others, and some just won't nest neatly together, even if they're technically compatible. So how do you choose?

While you're allowed to do more than one thing in your life, you can't do everything.

That's what this next exercise is for. It comes from Warren Buffett. As the story goes, Buffett asked his private jet pilot of many years something along the lines of "Do you have goals or aspirations other than continuing to be my pilot?" The pilot admitted that yes, he did indeed, but he hadn't been able to work toward them. So Buffett laid out this general process for him, in three simple steps.

STEP #1: LIST 25 OF YOUR GOALS

This exercise is about zeroing in on your top goals, but to get there, you first have to figure out all the goals floating around in your life and your head. So list them out, including both career and life goals. List at least twenty-five, but don't stop there if you've got more.

When I did this exercise for the first time, I was skeptical. Who has *twenty-five* goals? Then I started listing projects I was involved in. Résumé fodder I was working toward.

Positions I hoped to move into. Hobbies I wanted to explore. Skills I wanted to develop. My list went past twenty-five pretty quickly.

STEP #2: CIRCLE YOUR TOP 5

Next, really think about the whole list. Go over it. Search your soul. Circle your top goals, but *no more than five*.

You really have to be serious about deciding what your five (or fewer) most important goals are. Let me tell you, it's *not* easy. If you struggle to narrow your list like I did, I recommend using the "several stages of why" technique. For each goal, ask yourself why you want to achieve it. Then ask why again, and again, until you get to the root of the goal. When you first start asking why, your list will likely expand, but then there's a good chance you will find that several of your goals are really mid-level goals, with the same overarching goal above them. That top-level goal is one of the five goals you need to circle.

As an example, I had "gain programming experience" on my list. Why did I want programming experience? Because it moved me toward being on the data science team. Why did I want to be on the data science team? Because I wanted to work on clinical decision support—helping doctors make better medical decisions in complex situations. Looking back at my list, I realized I had a couple other mid-level goals like "gain programming experience." These goals weren't particularly important in and of themselves. They were important because they moved me toward the bigger, more unifying goal: working on clinical decision support. That helped me narrow the field quite a bit—instead of including all the mid-level goals in my top five, I included just the top-level goal: improving clinical decision support.

After you've weeded out the mid-level goals, if you're still struggling to pick just five top-level goals, you can temporarily put the list aside and either review or move on to the other exercises from this chapter. Also think about the things from the previous chapter—what makes us happy and the importance of passion and purpose. And if all else fails, just take your best shot for now, and schedule a reminder to revisit this exercise in a few months or a year.

STEP #3: AVOID THE OTHER 20

Now, take a good, hard look at the remainder—the other twenty goals on the list that are not in your top five. Remember these, because, according to Warren Buffett, you are to *avoid them at all costs*. This doesn't necessarily mean throwing out all your mid-level goals. But it does mean relegating them to their proper place: only of value in service to one of your chosen top-level goals, not in and of themselves. Remember the hierarchy of goals. Sometimes you can achieve a top-level goal without achieving all the mid-level or low-level goals below it. You don't want to get too hung up on lower-level goals.

This comes back to opportunity cost. Any time, money, or energy you spend on other goals is time, money, and energy you can't spend on your top five most important goals. If your attention and resources are divided between too many goals, you'll struggle to make significant progress on any of them. So get focused.

IDEAL VERSUS CURRENT TIME COMPARISON

This last exercise is about better understanding how you *want* to spend your time and how you *actually* spend your time. You probably already know that you're not spending all your time how you'd like, but you might be surprised by how much imbalance there is and where exactly the imbalances are.

In order to plan a change from how things are to how you want things to be, you first have to identify the gap between the two.

I recommend doing this exercise multiple times—once based on a day's worth of time, then a week, a month, and a year—because we all have some activities that we only do on a weekly, monthly, or yearly basis. For now, we're going to run through the exercise looking at the week level. Hang on to all your work here, because we will be using it again later in the book (Chapter 8).

STEP #1: FANTASIZE ABOUT YOUR IDEAL LIFE

First, take some time—ideally thirty minutes—and really envision what you want your life to be like five to ten years from now. Really fantasize. Don't worry about being "practical" or limiting yourself to what you already think is achievable. This is your *ideal* life. Of course, do keep things in the realm of reality. There's a difference between fantasizing about having a dragon as a pet and fantasizing about being able to take twelve weeks of vacation a year.

Set a timer for thirty minutes—I mean it. If you don't set a timer, you're probably not going to give this the time it needs. Then write down your thoughts, ideally in a journal or someplace where you'll be able to return to them later if you want. Again, I mean it. If you don't actually write these things down, you're not going to get as much out of the exercise.

Get detailed. Where are you living in this ideal life five to ten years from now? Who do you spend time with, and what do you spend your time doing? What do you do to earn money? Do you have new skills or hobbies? Have you reached a new level on anything you already do and enjoy? What does an average day look like? A normal week? Month?

STEP #2: ESTIMATE HOW YOU SPEND YOUR TIME IN YOUR DREAM LIFE

Now let's get even more detailed. Look over that dream life description. Create a table where you list out the activities in a typical week in that life and how much time you will spend on each one. You can do this with pen and paper or a spreadsheet. I prefer a spreadsheet because it makes it easier to sort and organize my list. It also gives me the option of turning the data into a pie chart as a visualization tool. If you opt for pen and paper, you'll need room for five total columns (activity name, ideal time budget, current time budget, difference between your ideal and current budgets, and a fifth column that will be added when we return to this exercise in Chapter 8).

You can leave out the day-to-day activities that are non-negotiable, like brushing your teeth or sleeping. But don't leave out things that can vary and impact your other time, like commuting, work, time with friends, time with your kids, reading, practicing ukulele, and so on. Use your own judgment here about what to include or omit. Prepping and eating food is a major planned activity for some, just a little piece of the day-to-day basics for others. Basically, if there's an activity that you think is going to remain static no matter what your life circumstances are, you don't need to include it.

There are 168 hours in a week. Subtract out sleeping (about 56 hours, if you average 8 hours a night) and the non-negotiable basics, like pooping, clipping your toenails, getting dressed, showering, and so on—call that another 2 hours a day, or 14 hours a week. That leaves you with about 98 hours per week to allocate. (This number may be higher or lower for you, depending on what you include as non-changeable, routine activities.)

If your list of activities is very long, group them into categories. If you have fifty different things in your list, it's hard to take all the information in, and it will be difficult to compare it to your current reality later (Step #4). Ideally, you won't have more than ten or so items in your list. Here are some common categories you might want to use:

- Work
- Relationships and social time
- Health/fitness/wellness
- Hobbies
- Fun/recreation
- Chores

If there is a specific activity that takes up a lot of time or that is particularly important to you, you may want to keep it on its own, even if it fits into one of these categories. For example, if you want to spend a significant amount of time doing a specific hobby, it could be helpful to keep that separate from the general "hobbies" bucket, so that you can more easily compare your ideal and current time allocations.

If you'd like, once you've finished your list, you could turn it into a pie chart, so you can easily visualize the proportions of how you want to spend your time.

STEP #3: RECORD HOW YOU SPEND YOUR TIME NOW

Now do the same thing with your current life. List how you actually spend your time right now.

Be very detailed here, and be realistic. Actually take a week and document how you spend your time, leaving out all those things you chose to leave out in the breakdown of your ideal life. Make sure it's an average week—doing this while on vacation wouldn't make the exercise very accurate. You should group your activities as you did in Step #2 for your ideal life, but you may need to add a category or two if there's something you spend time on now that wasn't on your "ideal" list at all.

In another column in your table, record how much time you currently spend on each category. As in Step #2, you can turn this information into a pie chart if you'd like.

STEP #4: COMPARE THE TWO

Analysis time. Compare the numbers for your ideal life and current life. Create another column in your table and list the difference in hours for each category.

Where are your mismatches? Are there any places where your reality actually matches your dream life? If you're using a spreadsheet, try out different sort methods, like by biggest current time allocation, by biggest ideal time allocation, or by biggest gap between current and ideal.

Highlight or mark any items from your dream life that are missing from or don't get enough time in your reality. These are the things you should try to do more of. Start thinking about how you could add these things into your life. What can you give up to make time for these things?

Then, using a different color highlighter or a different type of mark, identify activities in your current life that are not included in your dream life, or that get significantly less time in your dream life. Unless you want to incorporate these into your concept of a dream life, these are things you should try to eliminate or do less of. Start brainstorming how you could do that. Are they optional activities you can just eliminate, like watching TV? Will you have to hire someone else to do them, like chores? Or will you have to replace them with something else, such as replacing a job you don't like with a different money-making activity?

There are a number of ways to correct the imbalances between your ideal and current time budgets. Search for quick wins. Making a complete career change will probably take a lot of work, while decreasing TV time may be fairly easy. Or maybe you could talk to your boss about shifting your focus to the activities you enjoy most at work, which will help you feel more balanced even if your overall work hours remain the same. If you feel overwhelmed or unsure of what steps to take next, a coach can be a good idea, as they can help you create an action plan.

Now that you understand the gaps between your reality and your dream life, you can refine and make your goals more specific.

Current to Ideal Time Comparison

	Ideal (hrs/wk)	Current (hrs/wk)	Difference (Ideal-Current)
Office Work	0	45	-45
Teaching Sailing	25	0	+25
Building Furniture	10	0	+10
Commuting	5	5	0
Relationships and Social Time	14	4	+10
Family Time	20	8	+12
Exercise and Wellness	7	4	+3
Household and Home Chores	7	12	-5
Recreation	10	20	-10

This is the amount of change to make to get from current all the way to ideal

Ideal to Current Time Comparison

Ideal

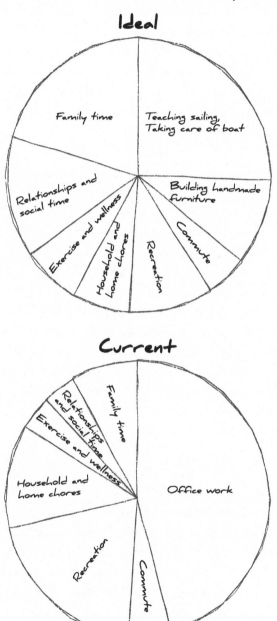

Current

CLARIFYING YOUR GOALS TAKES WORK, BUT IT'S WORTH IT

Doing these exercises takes time and energy. But in return, you can better understand your purpose, your goals, and yourself. You learn more about what you want, and you take one step closer to getting it. And bonus: the process can be fun! Who doesn't like fantasizing about their dream life and learning more about themselves?

If you've never done something like this before—or if it's been a while since you've done it—just give it a try. While you do need to take these exercises seriously and set aside a decent chunk of focused time to do them, they don't take *that much* time or work. For one night, skip your TV show, or order takeout instead of cooking, or let the dishes sit in the sink for a little longer. Make one of these exercises your priority that night. Do this to work through them all, because they'll pay off in the long-term. You don't need to do all of them at once. Spacing them out can help keep you in the right mindset of forward-thinking improvement. Also, these things aren't a one-time activity—you should return to them periodically throughout your life—so there's no point rushing through them just to finish.

You now have strategies for how to actually create your long-term goals. You might still be stuck in a boat in the middle of the ocean, but now you know how to use the night sky as a map—you know what general direction to head. The next step is to start navigating toward your destination. Your purpose and goals are your compass, but using that to navigate—actually making the small decisions that will get you to your destination—can still be challenging. A process helps. That's what we'll discuss next.

CHAPTER 6

—

USE A PRACTICAL PROCESS FOR DECISION-MAKING

If you can't describe what you're doing as a process, you don't know what you're doing.

—W. EDWARDS DEMING

As a doctor, a big part of my job is problem-solving and decision-making. A patient comes to me with certain symptoms, and my job is to figure out what's wrong (first big decision) and how to fix it (second big decision). It's simple in theory, but challenging in practice. The problems and solutions are often complicated, continually evolving, and time-sensitive. There's also a lot at stake—sometimes it's literally a matter of life or death.

It's a lot of pressure. So how do I consistently make the best choices I can for my patients without freaking out every time?

I follow a repeatable process.

Step #1: Decide How Much Time, Effort, and Resources to Spend on the Decision

I start by reviewing the case and creating a rough estimate of how much time, effort, and resources I should be spending on the decision. If I've been called into the hospital for an emergency, for example, I'll probably need to make my decisions more quickly than if a patient scheduled a routine appointment a month ahead of time. Or if a patient is experiencing worrying or unusual symptoms, I might need to take more time to be extra certain of my decisions, compared to a patient where everything points to a common and minor problem.

Step #2: List What's Important

Next, I review the patient's history and collect information about their symptoms, creating a list of everything that's important to the diagnosis. Sometimes the patient will provide detailed information, and sometimes all I have to go on is a vague "My back hurts."

Step #3: Look for a Clear Winner

From that initial information, I generate a list of all the realistically possible issues, deliberately casting a wide net. Within this list, I look to see if there's an obvious front-runner. If there is a way to quickly and easily confirm the front-runner option as the right diagnosis (or not), I will do so.

Step #4: Thin Your Options

Sometimes I end up with a diagnosis after Step #3. In most cases, though, I don't. At this point, I start whittling possibilities down. I ask the patient targeted questions to eliminate or confirm a particular issue and zero in on the right diagnosis. I look for additional information that is easily available (such as outside records, prior testing, or new tests that are inexpensive and quick). At this stage, the goal is to narrow the list in the way that is least expensive and least invasive for the patient. If I have twelve options and a different $800 test to confirm or deny each one, running all twelve tests isn't likely to be the best strategy, but my approach might vary depending on the urgency and severity of what is going on.

Step #5: Gather More Information

Once I've narrowed the list down, if there is still not a clear answer, I will then consider more expensive, more involved procedures—like CT scans, biopsies, and so on—in order to come to a final diagnosis. I may also review medical references or consult with colleagues and specialists to gather the information I need to make my final decision.

Step #6: Make Your Bet

Once I've reached an appropriate level of confidence given the circumstances of the situation, I make my diagnosis. I put a stake in the ground here. I document what I think is going on and tell the patient in detail what I think—and how confident I am about it.

Steps #1–#6: Round 2

With a confirmed diagnosis, I then move my attention to the second big decision: what to do about it. I go through all the same steps again. I decide how much time, effort, and resources to dedicate to this decision (Step #1), adjusting based on the diagnosis and circumstances. I list what's important (Step #2) in picking a treatment: effectiveness of the treatment, cost, potential risks and side effects, patient values (e.g., do they want to minimize suffering or prolong the length of their life at all costs?), and so on.

I then gather all the possible options and look for a clear winner (Step #3). Sometimes there's an obvious choice—such as a treatment that is 98 percent effective with almost no meaningful downsides. Other times, there are a lot of tradeoffs to consider. One treatment might be very effective but have several risks, while another treatment is less effective but carries almost no risk. I must then assess the options and narrow the list (Step #4). Again, I might consult with colleagues and specialists or review some medical studies to gather more information, and I will discuss the options with the patient so I can include their preferences and goals in the decision-making (Step #5). Eventually, we make a final choice (Step #6) based on the patient's particular circumstances.

Step #7: Evaluate

As the final step of my process, I evaluate the outcome of my decisions. Was the diagnosis correct? Did the treatment work? If the outcome isn't what we wanted, was there something I could have done differently, or did I make the best decision I could with the information available to me?

This process isn't particularly revolutionary, but it's incredibly important. By having a process, I can avoid missing important details. The process provides a framework to sort through multiple options with different risks and benefits. Essentially, while every patient and situation is different, the process keeps me from reinventing the wheel each time.

To appreciate how important a process is, simply imagine what would happen if I *didn't* use this process. Let's say you come to me because you've been having frequent stomachaches. Without a process, instead of first diagnosing the problem, I might jump straight to a solution and offer you antacid medication. Then, a couple of months down the line, the stomachaches still haven't gone away. We finally run more tests and discover that you have gallstones. You need surgery, not antacids, and we've lost valuable time in treating the problem.

Or maybe you come to me because your ankle has been bothering you. To figure out what's wrong, I order every test I can. We do x-rays, blood work, a CT scan, and an MRI. Turns out it's just a mild strain. You leave the hospital with some Tylenol and a bill that makes your eyes pop out of your head.

Clearly, there's a lot of value in having a process. This is true not just in the medical world, but for decision-making in general. Why should you approach your major career, education, or other life goals with less rigor than you expect your doctor to bring to addressing your sore ankle? If you approach your decisions with a process, you will be able to make better decisions and can also constantly improve and fine-tune your decision-making over time.

WHAT A BAD PROCESS LOOKS LIKE: PROS AND CONS LISTS

Whether you realize it or not, you probably already have a process for making decisions. If you're like most people, your current process probably involves making a pros and cons list, sometimes carefully, sometimes as just a rough brainstorm in your head. Pros and cons lists are a popular and often-recommended decision aid. They can help you see, side by side, some of the merits and drawbacks of various options you are comparing. Unfortunately, not all processes are created equal, and these lists are prone to critical errors. As author Annie Duke, who writes about decision science, says, "If you wanted to create a decision tool to amplify bias, it would look like a pros and cons list."[34]

Our cognitive biases hugely influence what items, and how many items, we think of for a pros and cons list. For instance, the status quo bias will make us list more positives for whatever the current state of affairs is and more negatives for anything new. The peak–end rule means we're most likely to list things related to the peaks or end of any prior experience. A pros and cons list also reinforces the distinction bias, encouraging us to consider and weigh small differences that don't really matter. It can also magnify a number of other biases we haven't even talked about, like confirmation bias (our tendency to search for, remember, and focus on information that fits our preconceptions, even if we are not aware of those preconceptions) and anchoring bias (our tendency to put too much emphasis on the first piece of information we receive or recall, rather than on the most important information).

Basically, any bias that affects your thinking is going to affect what you write down on your pros and cons list. When the "right" answer jumps out at you after completing your list, you may think you're making a logical and impartial decision, but really what you've done is rehearse and reinforce your preconceptions and biases.

---

34   Annie Duke, How to Decide: Simple Tools for Making Better Choices (New York: Portfolio, 2020), 129.

What if you know these risks and take every care to be objective in how you make the list? Even if you could theoretically eliminate all your biases, pros and cons lists still make it very hard to see the relative importance of the items listed. The format of a pros and cons list pushes us to give the same "weight" to each item in our decision. On the page, each item takes up the same amount of space, so our brains tend to view them as equally important and equally likely to occur, even when that's not the case. Consider this example of adding Drano to your coffee.[35]

PROS	CONS
Fun to try new things	Probably will kill you
Adds new flavor to drink	Probably will have permanent internal damage even if you survive
May have tingly feeling or other new coffee experience	
Cheaper than flavored syrups per ounce	
Available at the hardware store when picking up stuff for the garage	

At a quick glance, it looks like the pros outweigh the cons—after all, there are five pros and only two cons. But the cons should obviously carry the decision. Drano in coffee is a terrible idea, regardless of how many pros you can come up with.

Now, this is an extreme example. If you actually made this list, I hope you would recognize the clear and overwhelming importance of the "death or permanent damage" consideration and not be fooled by the length of the pros list. But not every important negative consideration is going to be as

---

35 I used to use an example about drinking bleach. Unfortunately and amazingly, that became a politically loaded topic in 2020 despite having a pretty similar pros and cons list to this one.

obvious as "you'll die from this." If there's something that obvious, you wouldn't need the pros and cons list in the first place. In a truly difficult decision, if you have a twenty-item pros list and a twelve-item cons list, will you be able to see past your (now reinforced) positive bias and identify which items (on both sides of the list) actually have the greatest impact on your future well-being? Maybe. Maybe not.

There are ways you can reduce the problems of pros and cons lists, but honestly, it's not worth it. Rather than create a pros and cons list and then do a whole bunch of other work to make sure you're not reinforcing your biases, why not use a better process?

A BETTER PROCESS: A FLEXIBLE FRAMEWORK THAT MITIGATES OUR BIASES

The best decision-making process is one that guides us to evaluate options in a way that minimizes the effects of biases rather than magnifying them.

I've spent twenty years studying decision science. I've combed through the best science available, taken the evidence of what works (and what doesn't), and combined the most important pieces to create a simple, usable process of just seven steps. The steps are designed in a way to minimize the effects of our biases. Please understand that this process does *not* eliminate bias. Nothing can do that. The nature of inherent biases is that they are *always* there, whatever decision support we are using. What you should strive for is to *counteract* them. So beware of your biases as you work through the process. Just because you understand the biases now and have some strategies for dealing with them, it doesn't mean you are completely immune.

Your cognitive biases are ingrained in you, and you will still experience them. But by staying on guard for them—and using the process laid out in this chapter—you can make much better decisions and expect much better outcomes.

One more note on this process before we get started. When you hear the word *process*, you might think of dry, boring spreadsheets or a lengthy, formal system. That's not the case here. This process is simply meant to be a framework to guide your decision-making. It is general and flexible enough that you can tailor it to your needs and use it in any situation. Just because you're using a process doesn't mean you can't have fun with it.

So without further ado, let's break it down. I'll use my career change as an example.

STEP #1: DECIDE HOW MUCH TIME, EFFORT, AND RESOURCES TO SPEND ON THE DECISION

The first step is to ask yourself, "What is a reasonable amount of time, effort, and resources to put into this decision?"

It's easy to get sucked down rabbit holes of research, especially with how much information we now have at our fingertips. At some point, though, there are diminishing returns on new information. This goes back to the idea we covered earlier of satisficing versus maximizing.

$$\sim\!\sim\!\sim$$

Instead of trying to gather all the information, focus on gathering enough information, so you don't waste time and energy to get limited additional returns.

$$\sim\!\sim\!\sim$$

You don't need to set a specific time limit here. The idea is to match your effort to the scope of the decision. Are you picking out a new toothbrush? Buying a car? Deciding whether to move across the country? You might spend weeks researching a major move, but if you spend that much time picking out a toothbrush, you've gone wrong. In my case, a career change was a major decision in my life, so I knew I wanted to put a lot of research into it. At the same time, because I was dissatisfied with my current job, I was eager to start on a new career path. I didn't want to get stuck in the deciding phase, so I planned to make a decision within a couple of months. This didn't mean I was committing to actually changing careers within that time frame. I was committing to make the *decision* about the change within a couple of months, so I could then move on to planning and action.

STEP #2: LIST WHAT'S IMPORTANT

Next, list the factors that are important to you in your decision. Do this *before* you start seriously comparing your options, or else you might get misled by your biases. This step is especially important to decrease the effects of the distinction bias. Having a list of the things that really matter can help prevent you from getting distracted by small and unimportant differences.

When I decided to switch careers, I knew a lot of what I *didn't* want based on my engineering jobs, and I did the exercises from the previous chapter to zero in on those things I *did* want. I ended up with this list:

- Work that feels valuable to me—that benefits other people or the world
- Work that will continue to evolve, providing ongoing opportunities to grow and be challenged
- Job stability and security
- Working with interesting people
- Decent income
- Flexible location

If you have a lot of items on your list, think about their relative importance to each other. You don't need a fully ordered ranking of the items (though you're welcome to do this if you'd like), but consider dividing them into a top-tier, must-have group and a second-tier, nice-to-have group. For me, income and flexible location were important, but when I thought about the impact they'd have on my day-to-day happiness, I decided they weren't quite as important as the other factors. So I put them into my nice-to-have group.

Remember: if you discover something later in your research that's not on your list, you can always add it. Just make sure it's something that's actually important to you.

STEP #3: LOOK FOR A CLEAR WINNER

Once you have your list of considerations, you can begin looking at your options. Start doing some more detailed research. Get a rough idea of how each option stacks up against your list, particularly those top-tier factors, and look for a clear winner.

Is there an obvious answer? Does one option clearly outrank the others in all or nearly all your top factors? If so, you're done. Stop there.

There is no such thing as a perfect choice, but sometimes, there may be one clear best choice.

If you find a job that checks off everything on your list, don't turn it down just because the commute requires you to use a toll bridge or because you don't get stock options. Don't let things that didn't make your "important factors" list out-weigh the things that did.

For my career change, these are the options I was considering:

- Continue in engineering
- Return to school for an advanced degree in physics
- Go to graduate school for robotics
- Go to graduate school for environmental science
- Open a martial arts gym in Portland, Oregon
- Do freelance web design

- Go into medicine

There wasn't a clear winner from this list for me. Every option met at least some of my key factors, and several checked off most things on my list. No worries—on to the next step.

STEP #4: THIN YOUR OPTIONS

Most of the time, there's probably not going to be a clear winner, so the next step is to narrow the field. With most decisions, you're probably starting with ten or fewer options. After thinning your options, you should be able to narrow that down to three to five. The goal is to eliminate the options that aren't real contenders so you can focus your time and energy researching just the top choices.

Start by looking for clear losers. Even if there's not a clear winner, there are probably one or more options that are clearly worse than the others. If so, eliminate them!

Don't waste time and energy on options that you already know aren't the best choices.

Another way to approach this is to separate your options into two tiers: top tier and second tier. Everything that falls into the second tier? Ax it! For me, I had three options on my career list that were pretty clearly backup options: continuing engineering, returning to school for physics, and doing web design. These were all things I had previously done, so I knew I could do them and get paid for them, but they didn't give me a sense of meaning. They were clearly second tier for me, and it was not worth taking additional time or energy to consider them. They continued to exist as backup plans, but I wasn't going to do any work to develop them unless my other options didn't work out.

If you can't identify any second-tier options, or you still have too many options left over after getting rid of the losers, you can try a decision bracket, in which you do one-on-one choice comparisons. Put your options in a list, in any order, and assign a letter to each one: A, B, C... (These aren't rankings, just designations.) Then run a bracket. Put A versus B, C versus D, E versus F, and so on. If you have an odd number, then the last option in the list gets a bye in the first round. Pick a winner from each matchup, and move it to the next stage.

Important note: The distinction bias pops up whenever we do direct comparisons, so be on the lookout for it. Keep your list of important considerations handy. The winner of each matchup should be whichever option fits that list better.

Once you go through all the matchups, do another round with the winners from the first round. Keep doing that until you get to a final matchup or a single champion. If you get all the way to a single choice, you may have your answer right there. While you may not have directly compared all your options, it doesn't matter. If you prefer B to A and A to G, then you already know that you prefer B to G—you don't have to compare them directly. If you can't decide in a particular matchup, circle it and let it go for now.

Run all the comparisons you can, then look at what you have left, including both options from any circled matchups. You can mix and match head-to-head comparisons to try to eliminate more options, or if you've successfully narrowed the field to three to five options, you can move on to the next step of the process.

Most people have a reluctance to discard options, but if you are ever going to make a choice, you have to do it. Be honest with yourself, and be ruthless. Don't cut things just because you feel pressure to decide, but *do* cut things that you're only holding on to because you want to "keep your options open" or you think you might change your mind later.

It is *always* possible your preferences will change in the future. So are you supposed to just never make any decisions? Of course not! You make your decisions based on everything you know and want now. If that changes in the future, then you make a new decision at that future time. When you're making a decision, don't waste time and mental energy repeatedly reevaluating options you've already judged as inferior on your current key considerations.

Decision Bracket

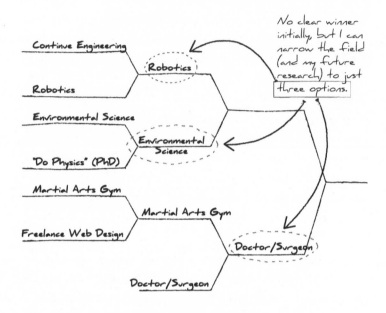

Continue Engineering
Robotics — Robotics

Environmental Science
"Do Physics" (PhD) — Environmental Science

Martial Arts Gym
Freelance Web Design — Martial Arts Gym

Doctor/Surgeon — Doctor/Surgeon

No clear winner initially, but I can narrow the field (and my future research) to just three options.

STEP #5: GATHER MORE INFORMATION

Once you have a narrowed field of choices, all of which score highly on many or all of your key considerations, you can dive into a more detailed investigation. In my case, after eliminating my second-tier options, I had just four options I needed to investigate more thoroughly: robotics, environmental science, martial arts gym, and medicine. So the next question is how to research most effectively.

Let's say you want to pick a movie to watch tonight. Should you watch two-minute trailers for each film you're considering, or look at the Rotten Tomatoes ratings? What if you had to pick between chef's menu A and chef's menu B for dinner tomorrow? Should you read the menu descriptions? Or would you be better off with a randomly selected review recommending one or the other without telling you what either option actually is? If you're like me and the vast majority of our fellow humans, you'd probably rather watch the movie trailers and review the menus yourself. I'm sure there are some highly rated movies you ended up not enjoying, or poorly rated ones you appreciated for your own reasons. Similarly, you know what kind of food you like. We all have our own tastes, so using our own intuition or imagination to predict whether we'll enjoy the movie or meal seems like a far better strategy than trusting random strangers' recommendations.

Well, it turns out that conclusion is dead wrong. There's a ton of research behind this.[36] Again and again, a random stranger who has gone through the experience we're considering is better than our own imagination at predicting our response to that experience. From which movie to watch, to which city to live in, to what car you'll be happiest with, to which menu you'll like more—you're better off trusting the recommendations of people who have already had the experience than trying to predict for yourself how you'll like it.

I know what you might be thinking: "That may be true for a lot of people, but not me. I know what I like, and it's not always what's popular." This is one of the ways the peak–end rule distorts our thinking. We remember all those times when we picked a winner that everybody else thought would be a dud, or when we hated something that was widely popular, but we fail to recall the vast majority of the times where we liked something about as much (or as little) as most other people did. We remember all the times we departed from public opinion precisely because they are less common expe-

---

36   See Daniel Gilbert, *Stumbling on Happiness* (New York: Vintage Books, 2006), particularly Chapter 11, "Reporting Live from Tomorrow."

riences. Though it can be a hard pill to swallow, the truth is we're not as unique as we like to think, and our imaginations are crappy simulators of reality. If a movie has an 18 percent rating on Rotten Tomatoes, chances are you're not going to enjoy it, even if you liked the trailer. And while something might not sound great to you on a menu, if the people who have actually eaten it loved it, you probably will too.

So, once you've narrowed your options, you actually do want to farm out some of the decision. You want to get advice from people who have already made the choice you're working through and have experience with one or more of the options you're still considering. If you're thinking about moving to a certain neighborhood, who better to tell you what it's like than someone who has lived there? Or if you're thinking about becoming a journalist, who better to talk to than an actual journalist? You can still gather your own information— watch the trailers, read the menus, and so on—but you should also weight other people's experiences and recommendations more highly in your decision.

Obviously, this strategy has some limits. You shouldn't blindly follow other people's recommendations without considering your personal preferences at all. If you legitimately hate mush- rooms, I'm not saying you should order a mushroom dish just because other people liked it. Other people's experiences show you what the reality will be far more effectively than your imagination can, but you still need to decide whether that reality is something you want. The bigger the decision, the more important this becomes.

For example, when I imagined running a martial arts gym, it seemed so cool. I have a black belt in Shotokan karate, and martial arts had a huge impact on me when I was a farm kid learning the basics in the elementary school gym. It gave me confidence and taught me self-discipline. I liked the idea of having that kind of impact on kids, and I thought it would be fun and low stress to spend my days doing something I enjoyed so much. Then I started reading about what running a martial arts gym was really like, from the perspective of gym owners. It turns out that teaching kids karate is only a small part of the job. The vast majority of the job is running a business—renting a space; hiring, training, and paying staff; doing advertising; coordinating travel to tournaments; dealing with frustrated parents; and on and on. Plenty of people enjoy doing all of that, but I knew I wouldn't be one of them.

Something similar happened when I did more research into robotics. I'd pictured myself working on cool, high-impact projects, like prosthetics, but when I looked into the reality of a robotics career, I discovered that those jobs were few and far between. Chances were, I'd end up working on projects similar to the ones in my engineering job, where I wouldn't be able to see my impact.

If I'd trusted my own imagination, I very well might have decided to open a martial arts gym or pursue robotics, and I quickly would've been disappointed by the reality of my day-to-day work. At the same time, if I'd asked roboticists or martial arts gym owners, "Do you recommend this career?" many of them would have said yes, but they would have said yes based on their own personal list of what's important in a career. I needed to know their opinions, but part of what I needed to understand was not "Is this good for you?" but rather "What is this like for you?" so I could better understand what it would be like for me. Gather as much information as you can from people who've actually gone through your decision, while always keeping your list of what's important front and center.

STEP #6: MAKE YOUR BET

After gathering as much useful information as you reasonably can, keeping in mind the rough time limit you set for yourself, it's time to stop researching and deliberating and make your decision. This step is the hardest in the process for many people. You may want to keep researching until you can be 100 percent certain of your choice. But remember: *all* choices are made in uncertainty.

~~~

No amount of effort will guarantee that your choice turns out well, and no choice will guarantee your future happiness and well-being.

~~~

Any decision might turn out better or worse than planned due to influences that are entirely outside of our control. That can be an anxiety-inducing thought, but also a freeing one. Because there is no perfect option, you don't have to lose sleep and increase stress over figuring out the perfect car to buy, the perfect job to take, or the perfect apartment to rent.

The stakes and certainty of each decision will vary, but every decision is a bet. Low-stakes, high-certainty decisions are the most comfortable for us. For instance, choosing between a quiche and a muffin at a place where you have always loved the quiche but the muffins are usually too dry is a pretty easy decision. As the stakes and uncertainty rise, with lots of unknowns at play, the decision gets more uncomfortable and difficult. How do you weigh having the military pay for your college education against the small but disastrous risk of getting killed by an IED during an overseas deployment? How do you decide to have children or not? How do you pick the right career path out of so many options?

First, stop trying to achieve a certainty that just doesn't exist. Instead, work to estimate how likely different outcomes are. You already do this in a binary sense, where you determine that one thing is more likely to occur than another, or this option will turn out better than that one. Take this a step further by putting actual percentages on the various outcomes, based on your past experiences and all the information you have. Say you've been offered a new job. Considering what you're looking for in a job and what you know about the position, what's the chance taking this job would make you happy—20 percent, 50 percent, 80 percent? You can relax a little—the numbers *can't* be perfectly accurate. Studies show that simply by assigning "best guess" percentages to possible outcomes, people increase the number of both alternatives and roadblocks that they consider in making a decision, and each of those factors has been independently shown to increase your chances of reaching your goals.[37]

---

37 J. A. Swets, R. Dawes, and J. Monahan, "Psychological Science Can Improve Diagnostic Decisions, *Psychological Science in the Public Interest* 1 (200): 1–26; B. Mellers, L. Ungar, J. Baron, et al., "Psychological Strategies for Winning a Geopolitical Forecasting Tournament," *Psychological Science* 25, no. 5 (2014): 1106–15; U. Haran, I. Ritov, and B. A. Mellers, "The Role of Actively Open-Minded Thinking in Information Acquisition, Accuracy, and Calibration," *Judgment and Decision Making* 8, no. 3 (2013): 188–201.

In my career decision, I was down to two options: environmental science or medicine. Environmental science felt valuable to me and was a field with a lot of growth potential. I also knew several interesting people involved in environmental science. Medicine also felt very valuable, and it was a job I could do just about anywhere. In addition to paying well, it came with a lot of job security. I was clearly making rough estimates. I felt that job security, pay, potential coworkers, and all the rest gave either a high shot at turning out well, but medicine seemed like the more solid of the two. I estimated that a job in medicine had about an 85 percent chance of turning out really well for me and environmental science around 70 percent.

While every decision is a bet, you don't have to go all-in on every decision, and you can hedge your bets by taking steps to minimize the downsides of your decisions. You can rent before buying a house in a certain neighborhood. You can foster a dog before deciding to adopt. In my case, I wasn't quite ready to put everything in the pot, so I decided to start with a smaller bet. I took evening classes to get certified as an EMT, then quit my engineering job and got two part-time jobs in the medical field. I got one job doing non-emergency ambulance and wheelchair transport, and I also worked as a lab tech at the local medical university. This small bet served a dual purpose. First, it was an experiment. If I discovered I couldn't emotionally handle being around sick and injured people all day or I wasn't interested in the work, I could switch paths before investing too much time, money, or energy. Second, if the bet turned out well, these positions would be major boosts to my résumé, putting me a few steps closer to becoming a doctor. Simultaneously, I hedged my bet by also applying to an environmental science PhD program. If my small bet on medicine went south, I had a backup plan.

No bet is a sure thing. Even with a 98 percent likelihood of something turning out how you expect, there's that 2 percent chance it won't. All you can do is give yourself the best odds you can, given the information reasonably available to you. If you consistently make smart bets—bets with odds better than fifty-fifty—statistically, you'll win more often than you lose. Your happiness will go up more than it goes down, and that's a winning strategy in the long run.

STEP #7: EVALUATE

The best poker players analyze the outcomes of their past bets in order to refine their future bets, and you should too. If you end your decision-making process at Step #6 and never take the time to evaluate how the decision turned out, you won't be able to correct course if needed, let alone improve your skills. Evaluate the outcome and the decision to make sure you're on the right path, headed toward the big goals you outlined in the previous chapter.

In evaluating your decisions, you need to recognize that a good outcome doesn't necessarily mean a good decision, and neither does a bad outcome necessarily mean a bad decision. If you drive through a red light and don't get into an accident or get a ticket, it doesn't mean it was a good decision. You just got lucky. Likewise, if you drive through a green light and get T-boned, that's obviously a terrible outcome, but it doesn't mean you should stop at every green light you see in the future. Because decisions are bets and the future is uncertain, there's always the chance that you'll simply get lucky—or unlucky.

So in analyzing your decisions, look at both the bad and

good outcomes. For the good outcomes, ask yourself, "Did I come out ahead here because I made a good decision, or did I make a bad decision and get lucky?" If the former, keep doing what you're doing. If the latter, then you should make a different decision in similar situations in the future. Hoping for luck is not a reliable plan. For the bad outcomes, ask, "Did I come out behind because I made a bad decision? Or was it a good decision given the information I had access to at the time, and the result came out poorly because of luck or unforeseen circumstances?" If you didn't anticipate the bad outcome because you didn't have the right information, come up with a plan for improving how you gather information or estimate your odds in the future. If it really seems like it was just bad luck, then you should make the same decision in similar circumstances in the future, even though this one turned out poorly. It's important to be honest here. Don't use bad luck as an excuse, but don't beat yourself up for things you can't control either.

You can do this evaluation process mentally, but it's even better to journal it. When you make a big decision, write down the decision, the odds you estimated, and a short sentence or two about why. Later, when you know the outcome, write it down too. That way, you can spot bigger patterns and trends you might otherwise miss. For instance, maybe you consistently estimate 80 percent odds for both relationship and investing decisions. Then, when you look at the outcomes, eight out of ten outcomes for relationship decisions turned out just as expected, while only five out of ten turned out how you expected for investing decisions. That suggests you may need to reevaluate how confident you are in your investing decisions. Remember the growth mindset: you're learning and getting better at decisions all the time.

MAKE THIS PROCESS YOUR OWN

It's important to have a process to your decision-making so that you can practice and get better, but you don't have to follow my steps exactly. You can use this process as a rough framework and make it your own, adapting it to your situation. This isn't like a recipe for a soufflé where you need to follow exact amounts in an exact order and meticulously time the baking or you'll end up with something sad and deflated. It's more like making a smoothie. Throwing in certain ingredients and avoiding others will help lead to success, but you can experiment and find what works for you.

The goal here isn't to make perfect decisions. That's simply not possible. There's always a little bit of randomness and luck involved in our outcomes. All we can do is consistently make smart bets so that we come out ahead in the long run.

Adopting a process will help you make smart-bet decisions and is a *huge* accomplishment in your journey to make better decisions, so congratulations for making it this far! You're now ready to start turning your decisions into action. For many people, this can be the most challenging part of the process, but don't worry. If you've struggled to follow through on decisions in the past, it's completely normal and likely due to a couple more cognitive biases. We'll take a closer look at those biases—and how to counteract them—in the next chapter.

CHAPTER 7

—

FOLLOW THROUGH ON YOUR DECISIONS

Time is your friend; impulse is your enemy.

—John C. Bogle

I've had a guitar my entire life. I inherited it when I was a baby. At the time, I was too busy learning how to crawl to learn how to play guitar, but in middle school, I decided for the first time, "I'm going to learn how to play!" I started working my way through a *Teach Yourself Guitar* book but quickly got bored of practicing the same two chords and fingerpicking patterns. Then, in high school, I again decided I wanted to learn how to play it. For several days, I practiced, then the guitar once more sat in the closet gathering dust.

As I grew older, whenever I moved, I lugged the guitar along with me, certain that the next time I decided to learn how to play it, I'd actually follow through. I took it to college, where I kept it in my closet so I wouldn't have to keep explaining to people that I didn't actually know how to play it. After graduating, I took it to Chicago, then Washington, Oregon,

California, and back to Oregon. I still couldn't play it. Again and again, I'd decide that I wanted to learn how to play guitar, and I'd dive into lesson books and online videos, but it never lasted. I'd put the guitar back in the case and not open that case again for months or even years. The next time I did haul the instrument back out and tune it up, it was like I'd never tried before. It was like the first time, every time. I wanted to be able to play songs my friends and I could recognize and enjoy, but I never got past the basic chords or the roadblock of my fingers hurting all the time.

Maybe you can relate. We've all struggled at one time or another with following through on a decision. *I'll start tomorrow,* we think, but tomorrow never comes. It simply becomes today, and we once more push off taking action.

You turn your decisions into reality with action.

Making the decision is only the start. If you don't actually *do* anything, your decisions won't get you the results you want.

WHY IS IT SO HARD TO FOLLOW THROUGH?

We make a decision, say we want to do something, but then we don't actually do it. *Why?* Why is it so hard to follow through? Because we're human. We are creatures of habit, and change is difficult. It's far easier to keep doing what we've always done (there's the status quo bias again). Even when we desire a change or know a change is needed, it can be difficult to make the change actually happen. A big culprit in this inaction is a lack of urgency.

Intellectually, we know we have a limited amount of time on this earth. Eventually, we will die, and the opportunity for action will have passed. We are aware of our future death, but usually only in a vague, nebulous sense. In our day-to-day life, it feels like we have infinite time. *There's always tomorrow,* we think. And thus begins a never-ending cycle of procrastination.

Connected to this, we often don't consider or fully appreciate the downsides of breaking our commitment to ourselves. We don't think about our future self and how they'll feel about us not exercising, or not saving for retirement, or not making the effort to change careers, or not practicing guitar. We value the short-term rewards of not following through over the long-term gains we might otherwise get. We'd rather spend our time today doing something easy or fun than putting in the work to achieve something that may not pay off for many months or years.

~~~~~

If you struggle to follow through with your decisions, it doesn't mean you're a bad or lazy person. Your brain just has you focused on the wrong things.

~~~~~

Just as cognitive biases can interfere with how we make decisions, they can also interfere with how we take action on those decisions. Fortunately, we can move beyond our biases. With understanding of the biases at play and strategies to counteract them, you will get better at following through on your decisions. Two biases that commonly disrupt our ability to follow through are time discounting and the exponential growth bias.

TIME DISCOUNTING: WHY WE PREFER SHORT-TERM GAINS OVER LONG-TERM ONES

If someone walked up to you and offered you $100 right now, or $110 in one day, which would you choose?

Now, let's say the same person approached you and offered you $100 in thirty days, or $110 in thirty-one days? Which would you choose?

Financially, choosing the $110 is better in both situations, and maybe you think you'd wait the extra day both times. But ask yourself this: Would it be easier to wait that extra day in the first scenario or the second? Definitely the second, right?

That's time discounting in action.

WHAT IT IS, AND WHY WE DO IT

Time discounting is a bias that pushes us to take a known reward or benefit now rather than wait for a bigger benefit in the future. It's a bias that affects our behavior a lot, from procrastinating on projects, to failing at diets, to not meeting our savings goals.

That example about taking $100 right now or $110 in one

day? Even though you might think you'd wait for the $110, studies show that when faced with the real choice in the moment, the vast majority of people opt for the $100 right now.[38] But in the second scenario, $100 in thirty days or $110 in thirty-one days, the vast majority of us are more than happy to wait that extra day to get an additional $10. From an economic standpoint, these are the same scenario—would you be willing to wait one day for an extra $10? But we give different answers depending on whether we have an option to receive our reward right now or not. We write off the benefit to our future selves ($10 extra! For nothing!) for the feeling of getting something we want right away.

Being able to delay gratification is critical to achieving long-term goals, so why are our brains seemingly built to set us up for failure?

Imagine you live with a tribe that has to hunt and gather food every day to survive. Your family members and tribe mates get sick and die with a regularity that makes the average life span around thirty years. In this scenario, the possible long-term rewards of delaying gratification become a lot less important than getting what you can now. If you aren't confident you'll have enough to eat tomorrow, planning for the long-term future isn't worth a lot of time or energy. Some research suggests that poverty, and food insecurity in particular, increases the effects of time discounting, which makes sense. In the setting of extreme scarcity, what seems like a bad long-term decision from the outside may actually be quite logical and necessary for survival.

---

38 S. Frederick, G. Loewenstein, T. O'Donoghue, "Time Discounting and Time Preference: A Critical Review," *Journal of Economic Literature* 40, no. 2 (2002): 351–401.

Our life spans are far longer today, though, and many of us are fortunate enough to not have to worry about our short-term survival. So this evolutionary instinct can often work against us.

HOW IT IMPACTS OUR DECISIONS

Time discounting is powerful and insidious. We don't even think about it as we do it. We easily justify our choices in the moment, genuinely believing we'll follow through on our decisions in the future. But when we get to that future, it becomes our present, and we once more justify our choices in the moment.

We repeatedly choose immediate gratification over whatever bigger payoff might be at stake.

This bias alone goes a long way toward explaining why we don't save enough money for emergencies or retirement, why we fail at quitting bad habits and starting good ones, why we can't stick to restrictive diets, and why we procrastinate in general. It's easy to see how time discounting can affect our ability to follow through on decisions. I'll have a doughnut today and start my couch-to-5k plan tomorrow. I'll buy this item that brings me joy today, and I'll put $20 in the kids' college fund tomorrow. I'll read an extra chapter in my novel today and get consistent with practicing guitar tomorrow.

In each of these cases, I'm making three mistakes: First, I'm assuming that my motivation, willpower, grit, or whatever will be both different and stronger in the future than it is now. It turns out that the opposite may be true, because I'm practicing *not* doing the better or more important thing in the present. Second, I'm consistently overestimating the long-term value of what I want right now. All the things I'm choosing to do today bring me short-term happiness, but not much long-term fulfillment. And third, I'm underestimating the long-term value of starting sooner rather than later. We'll get into this idea more in the next bias, but time slips by quickly. It's easy to think you can always start tomorrow... until you run out of time.

HOW TO COUNTERACT IT: IMAGINE YOUR FUTURE SELF AS A GOOD FRIEND

As with all our cognitive biases, the first step in fighting time discounting is knowing it exists, but that knowledge isn't enough on its own. Time discounting often happens behind the scenes, influencing our thinking without us...well...*thinking* about it. The best strategy to use is one introduced in Chapter 5: involve your future self.

Imagine your future self as a good friend at your side. You can even take out your age-adjusted photo if you created one. If you take the quick reward, you get it but your friend gets nothing. If you pass up the quick reward, your good friend gets the big payoff. How happy will your friend be if you make a small sacrifice or effort for them to have a much larger benefit?

Think through all the different scenarios that could play out based on your actions today. For instance, imagine a future in which you stuck to your workout plan and got fit versus a future in which you decided to push snooze on your alarm clock each morning. Or imagine a future in which you consistently invested for retirement—a retirement where you could stop working, live somewhere beautiful, and travel frequently. Then imagine a future where you didn't invest for retirement. You're at the age when your friends are retiring, but you have to keep working. You can't afford much travel when you do take a vacation, and you have moved into a smaller and older home in order to save money.

Really picture the possible scenarios, then imagine a conversation with your future self in each situation. Ask them how they feel about whatever action you're about to take in the moment: press snooze or get up for a run; buy that shiny new toy or put money away for retirement. Chances are, they'll say sacrificing in the moment or making that small bit of effort is worth it in the long run.

KEY TAKEAWAYS

- You have a natural bias to favor immediate payoffs, even if the longer-term payoff would be bigger.
- You can help fight this bias by thinking about your future self as a good friend and really weighing the relative importance of immediate gratification versus your long-term goals.

EXPONENTIAL GROWTH BIAS: WHY WE UNDERESTIMATE THE POWER OF COMPOUND EFFECTS

For long-term results, what do you think is more important: quantity or consistency? Is it better to work out for an hour every day for a month, then take a month off and do it again, or is it better to work out for half an hour every single day with no breaks? Is it better to save $100 every month or wait until the end of the year and put away $1,200 in a lump sum? If the total amount of time you spend working out or the total you save is the same, does it really matter when you do it? Yes. In these scenarios, it's pretty easy to see how consistency pays off. If you take a month off of exercising, you could lose the gains you made. If you save every month, you can start earning interest on that money right away.

But what if the quantity isn't the same? Is it better, for instance, to practice a new skill sporadically for a total of fifty hours, or is it better to practice consistently for just twenty-five hours, say half an hour every day for fifty days? Now it starts to get a little tricky. Yes, consistency is important, but fifty hours is twice as much as twenty-five—surely that's better! Nope, not necessarily. If you add up all the time I spent practicing guitar in the previous decades, it was probably about fifty hours, but because it was so sporadic, I had to keep relearning the same skills I'd already studied. When I finally got serious about my guitar practice, I progressed much farther with twenty-five hours of consistent practice than I had in my entire life up to that point.

Consistency is critical, but we have a tendency to underestimate its importance due to the exponential growth bias.

WHAT IT IS, AND WHY WE DO IT

The exponential growth bias is our tendency to be bad at visualizing how effects or benefits compound over time. When we think about how something grows, whether it's money, a skill, our health, or whatever, we tend to think of it linearly. If we were to picture a graph showing the growth over time, we'd imagine a straight line, steadily going up at the same rate—one hour of practice = x amount of new skill gained. In reality, though, many effects in life are not linear, but compound over time, which means the sooner we start, and the more consistent we are, the more long-term gain we get, more quickly.

There is a (presumably apocryphal) story you may have heard that illustrates how much more quickly exponential growth adds up than we expect. The story usually goes something like this:

Many, many seasons ago, an emperor wanted to reward his councilor for aiding him in a great imperial success. The emperor offered his councilor amazing riches, but the councilor modestly said, "Thank you, but no such riches are necessary. I can take my payment in rice. On this chessboard, place one grain of rice on the first square, and I will take it to my family. Tomorrow, place two grains of rice on the second square, and I shall take that rice. On the third day, place four grains on the third square and so on, doubling the rice each day. At the end of the board, on the sixty-fourth day, I will take my last payment of rice, and we will consider the matter settled." The emperor thought this an odd but surprisingly inexpensive way to satisfy a good advisor and happily agreed.

If you've heard any version of this story, you'll know how this turns out: not well for the emperor. Even if you've already heard the story, take a guess right now: How many grains of rice would the emperor have to give the councilor on the final, sixty-fourth day? Don't do the actual math. I'm not interested in the correct answer here; I'm interested in the answer that feels right to you, based on your gut and, yes, your exponential growth bias.

Got your guess? Good. Now we'll go through the math. The sequence starts 1 – 2 – 4 – 8 – 16 – 32 – 64 – 128. We're already across a whole row of the chessboard, and things don't look too bad. Next comes 256 – 512 – 1,024 – 2,048 – 4,096 – 8,192 – 16,384 – 32,768. Okay, things are getting a lot more interesting now. Let's jump ahead. On day thirty-two (halfway through), there would have to be 2,147,483,648 *grains of rice*, or over 53 metric tons (about 116,000 pounds) of rice. By the final square, the emperor owes his advisor 9,223,372,036,854,776,000 grains of rice. That's over 500 trillion pounds of rice. Modern world rice production is about 500 million metric tons annually. By doubling daily, this clever advisor earned themselves (in just over nine weeks) over 400 years' worth of the entire world production of rice. And that's just the payment on the final day, not all the days combined!

Obviously, this is an extreme example, but compare your guess to the actual final number. How far off were you? I'm guessing quite a bit. This illustrates the point that we have difficulty appreciating and comprehending how massive benefits can get with compounding over time. While there aren't many opportunities in life to double our benefits every day, there are a lot of opportunities to compound our benefits. When those benefits don't have a clear numerical value, it's even more difficult for us to visualize.

In general, any time you're learning a new skill, there are compounding effects—the more you learn, the easier it is to spot your mistakes, refine your abilities, and get even better. To help in visualizing this, let's use skateboarding as an example. Let's also say you are starting with a skill level of ten. Tony Hawk's skill level on this scale has a lot more zeros on it, but it doesn't matter. Let's say, for you, with each hour you spend in focused practice, you get 1 percent better. How much of a difference will it make to practice daily versus every other day?

After one year of practicing every other day, because those 1 percent gains compound, you'll increase your skills by a total of 600 percent, or six times. So what would happen if you practiced every day? Twice as many practices in a year, so that should be at least twice as good, right? Twelve times better? Nope. Here's where our poor estimating of compound growth tricks us: The power of compounding is that with twice as many 1 percent gains, if you practiced every day for a year, you'd get over 3,700 *percent* better—or thirty-seven times better instead of six times better!

So, why are we so bad at appreciating the impact of compound effects? Because it's simply not an important skill for survival, and it's not the kind of thing we get clear, explicit examples of very often. In our day-to-day life, there are plenty of examples of things growing at a linear rate—work x hours, get paid y dollars; spend x hours knitting, get y rows completed. But we've never actually struck a deal with an emperor to double our amount of rice each day. It's hard to really grasp something that far outside our everyday experience.

Compound Growth

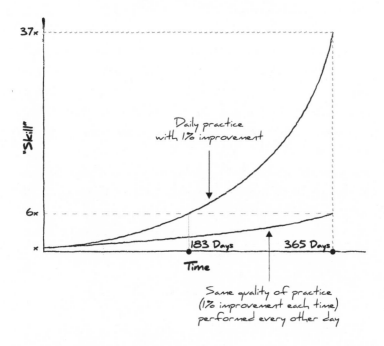

HOW IT IMPACTS OUR DECISIONS

Because of the exponential growth bias, we have a tendency to delay starting and a tendency to not remain consistent at activities that, if performed regularly, would result in compound growth.

One classic example of this is investing for retirement. You've undoubtedly heard that the sooner you start saving for retirement, the better—and it's true. But when you're in your twenties and don't have much wiggle room in your budget, it's easy to put off retirement investing in favor of more immediate gratification. *What's the big deal?* you might think. *I have decades. I'll just invest extra later.* With the compound growth of interest (or other investment gains), though, you'll have to invest substantially more in your thirties than if you'd started in your twenties.

We take the same mindset to all sorts of things in life. I don't feel like going to that leadership training. I'll just go to the one scheduled a few months from now. So what if I skip one workout? I'll just go on a long run this weekend. As the skateboarding example shows, though, the more consistent we are with our practice, the bigger the payoff. You might not care about skateboarding, but what about your graphic design skills, or speaking skills, or writing, drawing, counseling, or teaching? How much would it mean to you to increase your skills by six times in those areas? How about thirty-seven times?

～～～

We vastly underestimate the power of consistency. Small, steady action adds up to huge gains.

～～～

We can take this beyond money and skills too. We could apply it to happiness as a general concept. Journalist and author Dan Harris has quipped that meditating daily makes him about 10 percent happier (hence his book title: *10% Happier*). He's not transformed by bliss every day because of meditation, but his life is a little better and he feels a little happier if he does it consistently. Does that 10 percent effect compound? What daily activities of yours, even if they aren't bliss-inducing in the moment, make you a little happier, feel a little better about your life? What would it be like a year from now, and five years from now, if you actually did those things every day? How much better would your life be? How fast could the little daily gains from things like meditation compound into huge differences in your life?

HOW TO COUNTERACT IT: BUILD HABITS

As always, start by being aware of the bias. Understand that you have a natural inclination to underestimate the impact of compound gains. Similar to the time discounting bias, it can also be helpful to consult future you and see how they feel about how your compound gains have added up. But the absolute best way to combat this bias is to turn your actions into habits.

If you have to repeatedly make the decision to do a certain activity—practice skateboarding, invest a certain amount of money, whatever—then each of those decisions is a potential point of failure. Deciding to go on a run just one time is pretty easy. But deciding to go on a run three hundred times? Now it's starting to seem like it won't be such a big deal to skip a run here or there, and the more comfortable you are occasionally skipping your run, the easier it is for it to snowball, until you're rarely running at all.

When you make something a habit, you just do it without thinking. You take the decision effort out so you don't have that potential point of failure anymore. The best way to ensure consistency and thus benefit from those compound gains is to build a habit. Building habits is such a key lesson that I've dedicated all of Chapter 10 to it.

DECISIONS WITHOUT ACTION ARE JUST WISHES

Antoine de Saint-Exupéry famously said that "A goal without a plan is just a wish." The same might be said about a decision without action. You could be the best decision maker in the world. When faced with a list of options, you could avoid the common cognitive bias traps and zero in on the one with 99.9 percent chance of success. But if you don't follow through on that decision, putting in the work and taking the necessary action, it doesn't matter. The point of becoming a better decision maker is so you can start getting more of the results you want. That requires action. Decisions without action are just wishes.

Following through on our decisions can be incredibly difficult, especially because of cognitive biases like time discounting and exponential growth bias, which convince us that we'll always have time to take action later. Being aware of and taking steps to mitigate these biases can help, but if you really want to improve your follow-through, what you need is an actionable plan. In the next chapter, I'll take you through a general process for turning any goal or decision related to a goal into a plan you can use.

CHAPTER 8

TURN YOUR DECISION INTO AN ACTIONABLE PLAN

The way to build a complex system that works is to build it from very simple systems that work.

—KEVIN KELLY

A few years ago, I was asked to observe a board meeting for a small nonprofit. One of the leaders of the organization wanted suggestions on how the board could change its structure or its work to become more effective. The board was made up of volunteers—all intelligent, well-educated, invested people who wanted the organization to succeed. But I knew before the meeting even started that it was going to be a disaster.

The meeting, scheduled for two and a half hours (!), went more than an hour over the allocated time. There was a lot of cross-talking, with people's emotions out on the table. They went back and forth on some simple issues and a couple more challenging issues...and literally *no* decisions were made. *No* actions were taken. The only concrete action planned for the future was to meet again.

It was painful to sit through as an observer, and I couldn't imagine being a participant in one after another of such meetings. When I told the director my impression, he said, "That was actually one of their better meetings. It goes on like that even longer sometimes." I talked to a few of the board members, and the general feeling was that yes, the meetings were long, but it was necessary to get through the agenda. And it was true: they did get through the whole agenda in the meeting. So how was it possible that not a single decision was made, nor a single action taken? When I posed this question to the board members, half were mystified, and the other half thought it was only because they were dealing with important and complex issues.

I had another explanation. The reason I knew—before the meeting even started—that it was going to be a disaster was because I had a copy of the agenda. It had six or seven items on it, each a single line: "Discuss [topic]." And that's exactly what happened. The board members all mentally patted themselves on the back for accomplishing every item on their agenda. They did in fact *discuss* every topic. But because the agenda (the plan for the meeting) was so poorly designed, they didn't actually accomplish anything. It is true that sometimes the goal of a meeting *is* discussion, like community listening sessions where decision makers can hear what the people they serve think about an issue, but in this case, the meeting did not move the board any closer to their goals as an organization.

Moral of the story? You need a plan, and it can't just be any old plan. A plan is only effective if it moves you toward your goal. That means you need an *actionable plan*.

WHY YOU NEED AN ACTIONABLE PLAN

You've probably heard the saying: "Failing to plan is planning to fail." Lots of research supports the idea that having a plan increases your chances of success.

Big life or career goals are long, complex endeavors. There's typically not a simple path or a single clear action for you to take. Even if you know where you want to go, it's going to be difficult to get there without a plan. At best, you're going to be inefficient, and at worst, you're never going to get there at all. Having a plan is the difference between navigating in a general direction using the stars in the sky versus navigating with a GPS that shows you exactly where you are and the path you need to take to reach your destination.

Without clear action steps—specific things you can reasonably accomplish, right now—you may quickly be overwhelmed by the enormity of the goal. You won't know where to start or what step to take next, and so you won't do anything at all. Even if you're highly motivated to achieve your goal, like those board members were, you'll still be paralyzed into inaction.

When you make a big decision, like setting a long-term goal, you pick a destination. An actionable plan is your map for how to get there. It tells you exactly what action you need to take and when, and that greatly improves your chances of success.

DEFINE A SPECIFIC GOAL

The very first step is to define a specific goal you're trying to accomplish. At this point, if you're going through the book in order, you should already have some big goals in mind, but there's a good chance they're not specific enough to really plan around. To make a goal specific, establish a clear, measurable target and a deadline for achieving it.

This step is absolutely critical. If you skip it and jump straight to to-dos, you'll likely create a list of tasks that don't drive you closer to your goal. As you check off the to-dos, you'll feel as if you're making progress, but that's only true if what you want to accomplish is "finishing tasks." As an extreme example, if your big goal is to own a home, having a task list that says "get milk on the way home, call Mom, vacuum minivan before Saturday" isn't going to move you closer to your goal. Even if the task items are more clearly related to your goal, they likely won't be targeted enough to drive actual progress. That's exactly what happened with the nonprofit board. They were enacting their plan—discuss the topics on the agenda—but that wasn't moving them toward their big goals of keeping the organization growing and financially sustainable. They weren't making decisions, and they weren't defining measurable actions (let alone performing them).

~~~

You can't recognize whether you're on the right path if you don't know where you're trying to go. So make your goal specific.

~~~

Take the goal you're going to build a plan for, and describe it in as precise a way as possible. For example, instead of

"Own a home," you might rewrite that goal to something like "In five years, purchase a house that I can raise a family in."

BREAK THE GOAL INTO ACTIONABLE STEPS

Building the life you want can seem daunting. By breaking your goals down into their actionable steps, you can make steady progress without being overwhelmed.

Our big goals are almost always complex tasks. But every big goal is made up of many simple, doable tasks.

Start by listing mid-level goals you need to complete to achieve your top-level goal. To purchase a house, that might be: save for a down payment, determine your requirements for the house and location, perform the house search, and go through the buying process. Those goals are more manageable, but they're still not action steps. Your brain has evolved to conserve energy when it can. If you put "save for a down payment" on your to-do list, your brain will look at that and think, "There's a lot I could do to work toward that, but I don't know exactly what I should be doing right now. Sorting that out takes energy, and I already have shelter and food available, so I'm not going to waste any energy figuring it out."

So keep breaking the items down until you arrive at a well-defined action you can take at a specific point in time. Saving for a down payment requires that you (1) identify a realistic price range for what you plan to spend on the house, taking into account what you can afford and where you want to live, and (2) create and stick to a budget that includes saving for the down payment. You can break both of those steps up even further. Number 2 might become: (a) download a budget app, (b) review current expenses, (c) look for areas to save money, (d) determine how much money you can save each month for a down payment, and (e) set up automatic deposits. Those are tasks your brain can wrap itself around. They are things you can put on a to-do list and actually complete in a single day.

There is a danger here of overplanning, and depending on the goal, it may be too overwhelming to break it down into all its component parts like this. If so, chunk the goal based on timescales instead. Pick one of your big, long-term goals. What do you think you can realistically achieve in three years that will put you on the path toward that big goal? Write it down. Now think just one year out—what can you achieve in the next twelve months that will put you on the right track to achieving your three-year goals? Write it down again. Now, in the next month, what goals can you accomplish that will move you toward your one-year vision? Write them down. How about the next week—what can you do to start working toward your monthly goals? Now, final step: what can you do *today* to move you toward accomplishing your goals for the week?

Note that I did not say, "Sit down and plan out each of the next 365 days immediately." You need some flexibility here. Some things will take longer than you expect, and some things will go faster. Sometimes you'll get interrupted, or new opportunities will arise that put you on a different path, either a new way toward the same goal or toward entirely different goals. It's helpful to have target goals at the different timescales so if you get thrown off course, you can adjust and get back on track for your long-term goals. But it is a waste of time to do day-by-day planning months or even weeks in advance.

Breaking goals down in this way may seem overly simplistic, but this is how fantastically complex and long-term goals get accomplished. Want to send a rocket to Mars in four years? You're not going to get there by saying, "We need a rocket that works in four years." You get it by breaking it down into subprojects, sub-subprojects, sub-sub-subprojects, and so on, until you get to steps like "Today, install the valves in the propellant tank." It isn't rocket science in the normal sense, but it is those kinds of mundane steps that actually make a rocket go. And it is mundane steps today and tomorrow, and every day, that can move you from where you've been to where you want to be.

Actionable Plan

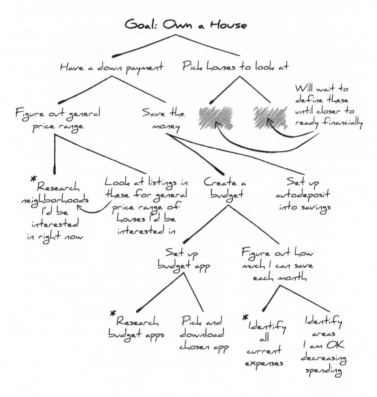

Goal: Own a House

- Have a down payment
  - Figure out general price range
    - *Research neighborhoods I'd be interested in right now
    - Look at listings in these for general price range of houses I'd be interested in
  - Save the money
    - Create a budget
      - Set up budget app
        - *Research budget apps
        - Pick and download chosen app
      - Figure out how much I can save each month
        - *Identify all current expenses
        - Identify areas I am OK decreasing spending
    - Set up autodeposit into savings
- Pick houses to look at
  - [shaded box]
  - [shaded box] ← Will wait to define these until closer to ready financially

*Next steps: <u>Specific</u> things I can <u>do</u> with what I already know and have.

CREATE CLEAR, SIMPLE RULES FOR YOUR ACTION STEPS

Now, for any of your action steps that are general or vague, create clear, simple rules. Remember that our brains are kind of lazy. They don't like spending energy if they don't have to. If you create clear rules, your brain won't have to think about what to do in various situations. It'll just do it.

If you have specific rules about what to do—and what not to do— you're more likely to stay on track.

This strategy can be particularly useful in building consistency around actions. Compare "drink less" and "don't drink at home on weeknights." They're both action items related to the same type of goal. However, "drink less" is vague and requires a lot of work to track. You'd have to keep a running tally of how much you've had to drink this week or month and compare it against your past consumption. In contrast, not drinking at home on weeknights is a simple, easy-to-follow rule. You still have the option of grabbing a drink with friends after work or having a drink with dinner on the weekend, but if you crack a beer open on Thursday evening at home, you know you've broken the rule. Minimal mental effort and a clear "in-bounds versus out-of-bounds" definition means this approach is much more likely to succeed.

You can apply this same concept to just about anything—exercising, saving money, and so on. You can even make clear, simple rules about completing the action steps of your plan. For instance, once you've defined all the individual action steps of a goal, you could make the rule that you will complete one item a day.

The more explicit you make your boundaries and rules, the less cognitive effort it will require for you to take action, and the more likely you will be to keep taking the next step in line—and moving toward your goal.

"I JUST DON'T HAVE ENOUGH TIME!"

EXERCISE: TIME–VALUE INVENTORY

When you create your actionable plan and begin working toward your goals, you may feel overwhelmed by how much there is to do. Even with your goal broken down into simple, easy steps, it still takes time to do those things and make progress. And time seems to be something we never have enough of.

Chances are, as you probably discovered in the "ideal versus current time comparison" exercise in Chapter 5, you're not spending your time exactly how you would like to. Now it's time to do another exercise: a time–value inventory that will help you begin spending more of your time how you want.

Pull out the list you created in Chapter 5 of all the activities you do and how much time you spend on each one. Now create another column for how important the activity is to you. You could use a simple "low, medium, or high" scale, or you could use a "strongly disagree, disagree, neutral, agree, strongly agree" scale, in response to the statement "This activity is meaningful to me." You could also use a 0 to 10 scale if you're numerically minded and want to really differentiate between the relative importance of your activities.

Look for all the places where there is a large mismatch between the time spent on an activity and its value to you: high-importance but low-time activities and low-importance but high-time activities. If you're doing this on paper, mark all the high-importance but low-time activities with a star, and mark all the low-importance but high-time activities with a down arrow. If you're using a spreadsheet, you can highlight the two categories with different colors.

Time-Value Inventory

For the biggest impact, focus on correcting large mismatches between how much you value an activity and how much time you spend on it.

	Ideal (hrs/wk)	Current (hrs/wk)	Difference (hrs/wk)	Importance
Office Work	0	45	-45	Low (3)
Teaching Sailing	25	0	+25	High (8)
Building Furniture	10	0	+10	Medium (6)
Commuting	5	5	0	Low (1)
Relationships/ Social Time	14	4	+10	High (10)
Family Time	20	8	+12	High (10)
Exercise and Wellness	7	4	+3	High (8)
Household/ Home Chores	7	12	-5	Medium (4)
Recreation	10	20	-10	Medium (5)

If those big mismatches are in categories that will take a lot of work and time to change (like a complete career change), you can also look for "quick wins" in other high-value categories.

This should already be sparking some ideas of how you might be able to shift some of your time away from your low-value activities toward your high-value activities. And there's probably a good chance that those high-value activities are things that support your goals and fit into your actionable plan.

For now, start small. Pick one low-importance but high-time activity. For the next week, take some of the time you normally spend on that activity and instead spend it on your actionable plan.

MAKE YOUR ACTION STEPS INTO HABITS

The final step is to turn as many action steps into habits as possible. This is another way to reduce the cognitive load and the energy required to stick to your plan.

In the next chapter, we'll go into detail about how habits work and how to create them. Right now, just identify which action steps you can turn into habits. With some goals, it will be easy to see how to turn the action steps into habits. For example, goals centered around skill development, like learning a language or how to play a musical instrument, require regular practice. "Practice twenty minutes a day" is the kind of thing you can easily structure as a habit.

For a goal like "purchase a house in five years," it's not always obvious how to turn the steps into habits. Many of the actions are one-time events. But you can turn the work itself into a habit. Your habit could be spending twenty minutes every day after dinner to work on whatever the current action step of your plan is, whether it's researching neighborhoods, creating a list of what you want in a house, or looking at listings to figure out your budget. You might also be able to build habits that support your mid-level goals. With saving money, for instance, you could create the habit that every time you enter a store, you check your budget on your phone to see how much money you can spend.

Even with a clear plan, you still have to actually *do the things* in the plan. The more action steps you can turn into habits, the more likely you'll be to follow through and achieve your goals.

NOBODY CAN ACHIEVE YOUR GOALS FOR YOU

We spend a lot of our early life being told what to do—by our parents, teachers, coaches, and other adults. Even as adults ourselves, we're frequently told what to do by family, bosses, even friends trying to be helpful. Being told exactly what to do can be comforting and easy, but when it comes to your goals, you need to take ownership. You need to tell yourself what to do, with an actionable plan. With a well-defined goal, specific tasks you can actually complete, and clear rules to follow, you can set yourself up for success.

You can get support and guidance from other people, and a coach can even help you formulate your actionable plan. At the end of the day, though, these are *your* goals, no one else's. You are the one who has to take action and do the work to achieve them. Habits are one of the best ways to ensure you stick to the plan and make steady progress, so in the next chapter, we'll look at how you can build habits that last a lifetime.

CHAPTER 9

AUTOMATE YOUR SUCCESS WITH HABITS

You will never change your life until you change something you do daily. The secret of your success is found in your daily routine.

—Darren Hardy

Quite a few years ago, I injured my back while skiing. Ever since, I occasionally get severe cramping pain in my lower back after a totally mundane activity, like reaching for a loaf of bread on the counter. The pain can last for days or even a few weeks, and it can completely disrupt my life. At its worst, it makes it hard for me to walk normally, to pick things up, or even put on socks.

I've known since the first few months after the injury that a combination of basic core strength and simple but regular stretching almost completely eliminates these episodes, and makes them much shorter and less severe on the rare occasions they do happen. With such a simple solution, you'd think I would never have to worry about these cramping episodes, but you'd be wrong.

While I'm pretty active, I've never been a dedicated stretcher or particularly excited about core work. I know I need to do these things, and I try, but in a pattern familiar to most people with fitness-related goals, I go through cycles. I start out highly motivated, doing my stretching and core exercises daily, but after a few months, other responsibilities creep in. I start to skip a day here or there, then a bunch, until there's no pattern or consistency left. Then I go for a Tupperware on the bottom shelf, and *twang*! I tweak my back again and spend the next two weeks hobbling around in pain. "I'm going to stretch and work my core consistently!" I vow to myself, and the cycle starts again.

I repeated that cycle for years, until something important changed. After having (again) grown inconsistent with my exercises, I once again threw out my back. The physical pain wasn't any worse than in past episodes, but emotionally, this one knocked me flat. It hit right before one of my younger daughter's basketball games. I could barely make it through the game, as a *spectator*. It was too painful to sit in any set position for even a couple of minutes, and standing still got uncomfortable pretty quickly too. I ended up having to slowly limp back and forth and lean on the gym wall throughout the duration of the game, which drew quite a few odd looks.

Then the next day, my daughter asked me to shoot hoops with her in the driveway. It was a perfect weekend day—sunny but not too hot. I had nothing else planned, and this was the first time she'd been really engaged in and excited about a team sport. There was nothing I wanted to do more at that moment than shoot around with her. But I couldn't. It hurt to walk, to turn, to stand up straight and reach, to bend. There was no way I could play basketball, even just to rebound for my daughter and pop up a shot now and then.

My daughter was very understanding about it, but I knew something had to change. Making a decision and a plan to do my stretching and core exercises wasn't enough. I needed to make these things into a habit that stuck.

THE POWER OF HABITS: HOW AND WHY THEY WORK

Staying on track toward your goals takes consistent effort. What knocks many of us off course is actually not the time or energy to do the needed tasks, but failing to account for the time and energy it takes to, time after time, day after day, figure out which tasks to do and decide to do them.

———

The less effort needed to decide whether to do something, when to do it, and how to do it, the more energy you'll have for actually doing the thing.

———

You can use habits to shortcut this process and save a lot of decision-making energy and time. That means you'll have more energy and time to actually complete the task, leading to more consistency. Consistency moves you through the steps of your plans and, in the right circumstances, increases your progress through compound effects.

Time and energy are two of our most valuable resources, and they're both limited. Have you ever had a tough day at work, where you had to make a lot of decisions and expend a lot of mental energy, and then when you got home and opened the fridge you couldn't decide what to eat because your brain was so fried? That's decision fatigue.

Fortunately, mental energy is a renewable resource. It's not gone forever if you deplete it (though if it's gone when you need it, it's still a problem). Time, on the other hand, is *not* a renewable resource. Once it's gone, it's gone. Do you really want to spend your time and energy making the same decisions over and over again, when you could instead automate those decisions with habits?

When you establish a habit, you're essentially using the default bias to your advantage. The decision (to do the activity and when) is made from now through forever. Changing the habit or not completing the action might take more mental effort than simply letting the default run its course.

So how do habits work? Every habit is a loop: stimulus (or cue), desire, behavior, reward. You've probably heard of Pavlov's dogs. Dr. Pavlov was a psychologist who, among many interesting discoveries, noted that if he sounded a buzzer[39] every time he fed his dogs, after a while, the dogs came to associate the buzzer with food so much that they would start salivating when the buzzer sounded, whether or not food was provided. The buzzer was the cue, which triggered a desire (or expectation) for food, which caused the salivating, which

---

39 Pavlov used a variety of stimuli in his experiments, including a metronome, a harmonium, a buzzer, and electric shock, but he didn't actually use a bell. The somewhat iconic image of Pavlov's bell comes from early translations of his work that incorrectly translated the Russian word for *buzzer* as "bell" in English.

the dogs associated with eating (the behavior), and then the food was the reward.[40] Our habits work the same way: cue, desire, behavior, reward.

The habit loop is neutral—it's not inherently good or bad, which is why we can have both good and bad habits. The same events in your brain that save you from having to think about how to use toilet paper and what direction to turn to find the flush lever also contribute to you automatically checking social media every time you're bored or "needing" a doughnut every time you sit down at your desk in the morning. By understanding the loop, we can work to break our bad habits and instead build loops that support our desired actions and goals.

With that in mind, let's now look at how we can begin creating the kinds of habits[41] that will drive us toward our goals.

---

40 In some research and many discussions, the term "reward" can mean either the large-scale prize (such as getting food) or the specific neurobiological response (like the squirt of dopamine in your brain that makes you feel good after getting the prize). In a practical context, the distinction isn't as necessary, so I'll use "reward" to refer to both the prize and the neurobiological response.

41 Some people prefer to make a distinction between routines and habits, with a habit being an unconscious response to a cue and a routine being a series of steps that may be built off of an initial cue but that require conscious effort to complete. The distinction can be important in psychology research, but for our purposes, I'll use the terms interchangeably to mean anything that decreases the friction and lowers the mental energy needed to complete a desired task.

Habit Loop

Cue:
The trigger: the signal you associate with getting the reward

Desire
Body and mind start anticipating and expecting the reward

Behavior
The thing you do

Reward
The in-the-moment happy feeling

FIND YOUR REASON

While habits will ultimately save you time and energy, creating a habit takes effort. If building good habits were easy, we'd all be doing it already. In order to get over the initial hump of effort required to establish a habit, you need to find a reason bigger than just wanting to do it.

The obvious reason is to get closer to your goals. This alone can be very motivating—obviously you care about your goals, or they wouldn't be goals. To make your goals as motivating as possible, identify the concrete outcome you hope to achieve and the *why* behind the goal. For instance, a goal of "get fit" might turn into "get healthy and fit enough to hike [concrete outcome] so I can spend time with my grandkids [why]." Or a goal of "save more money" could become "save money for a new laptop [concrete outcome] so I can more easily work remotely [why]."

If you're struggling to find a reason, try looking outside of yourself. Want to quit smoking? Imagine not being around for your kids or grandkids because of lung cancer. Imagine making your partner sick because of secondhand smoke. Quitting for your personal health can be a motivating reason, but even more motivating will be quitting for the sake of other things—and, most powerfully, other people—you care about.

With my stretching and core exercises, avoiding the painful cramping episodes seems like a good enough reason to make me build the habit, but it wasn't. For the habit to stick, I needed an even better reason. I found that reason the day my daughter asked me to play basketball with her and I had to say no. While she was outside in the sunshine shooting hoops, I sat inside and wrote a note to myself, which I now copy into the early pages of every new journal I start. It's a short paragraph about the beautiful weekend, how fired-up my daughter was, and how much I wanted to join her but couldn't because of the pain. It finishes with this observation: "I don't want to miss out on doing things with my kids (or things in general, but especially with my kids) because of pain or fitness." Stretching and doing core exercises regularly was all fine and good as a way to avoid pain, but the habit only really stuck once it sunk in as a way to improve my ability to be present for my kids.

Once you have your reason, you can begin changing a bad habit or building a new desired habit. There are two approaches you can take: modifying an existing habit loop, or creating a brand-new one. We'll start with how to modify an existing loop.

MODIFY AN EXISTING LOOP

Modifying an existing loop is useful for changing a bad habit, and it can serve a dual purpose: establishing a good habit while simultaneously eliminating the bad habit. First, identify the loop that exists: cue, desire, behavior, reward. The behavior will probably be the easiest thing for you to identify, since that's what you want to change, but you need to identify the entire loop in order to break it. The cue and reward are especially important to identify—the cue because it's the trigger for the behavior you want to change, and the reward because it's why you do the behavior.

Let's say every morning you eat a doughnut, and you want to break this habit. What activity triggers the desire for the doughnut? It could be related to thinking about checking your email, imagining your morning review of the project budget, or simply sitting down at your desk. For this example, we'll say it's sitting down at your desk. So, you sit down at your desk (cue), salivate (desire), eat doughnut (behavior), and get a squirt of dopamine that makes you feel good (reward). Simply deciding, "I'm not going to have my morning doughnut anymore," will be a hard decision to stick to, because you want the doughnut and the dopamine. The cue is still going to happen, which will trigger the desire, and the only thing that will keep you from not eating the doughnut is telling yourself no. As you probably know from life experience—and as lots of psychology research supports—that approach just isn't going to work, especially not long-term, because you have to exert that willpower every single time the desire hits.

Eliminating habits is incredibly difficult. Replacing an undesirable behavior is far more achievable.

Instead, once the cue and desire hit, you need to substitute a new behavior. This new behavior can be basically anything, as long as it's followed up with a reward. So with our dough-nut example, let's start with the reward. You want to find another way to trigger dopamine without eating a sugary treat, so what is the most pleasurable activity available to you during breaks at work? Maybe it's making a trip to the watercooler to chat, or taking a walk up and down the flight of stairs with the big window, or going outside for fresh air, or listening to a song that pumps you up. Get creative here, and find something that works for you.

Now that you have a reward ready, you can substitute a new activity. We're going to call this your new habit, even though it's really the whole loop that's the habit, not just the activity in the middle. There's a lot you could choose for your new habit, and it really depends on what you want to achieve. Maybe you want to get your least favorite work out of the way early, or maybe you want to immediately dive into the most productive thing you normally do in your first hour at work. You could decide to catch up on email, review reports from the previous day, take the next step on the week's major project, and so on.

Here's an example of what the new loop could look like:

"From now on, when I sit down at my desk (cue), I will set my phone timer for twenty-five minutes and review yesterday's reports (behavior). After that, I'll take a walk around the block (reward)." Now the same trigger—sitting down at the desk—will be associated with a new immediate activity (set the timer instead of picking up a doughnut) and the follow-through will be a behavior you want (focused work rather than eating a doughnut). The reward then provides a little dopamine hit just like the doughnut would have, reinforcing the habit. When you first start substituting the new activity, you're still going to feel the desire for a doughnut, but with repetition, your desire will shift to wanting to take your walk.

Modifying an existing habit loop still takes effort, but it's far easier and more effective than trying to eliminate a bad behavior without replacing it.

Modify a Loop

Sit down at desk

Cue

Salivate, anticipate some dopamine

Desire

Dopamine hit!

Reward

Take a walk around the block

Eat a donut

Behavior

Set timer and review reports

CREATE A NEW LOOP

You can also start an entirely new loop in order to establish a habit. This may not always be easier, but it is simpler, because there is no old habit to break. All you have to do is pick a cue, set your desired behavior, and then give yourself a reward.

The biggest mistake people tend to make when creating new habit loops is not picking a cue. That was one of my problems with my stretching and core exercises. I thought that as long as I was doing them every day, I was building a habit. So sometimes I'd do them first thing in the morning, sometimes I'd do them at lunch, and other times I'd do them in the evening, whenever I could fit them in. The result was I wasn't actually building a habit at all. A habit is formed by linking a cue and a behavior. The way I was doing it, there was no cue. I still had to think about and decide when to do the stretching and exercises each day. I could hold myself to the behavior for a while, but because I had to exert willpower and energy to do it, it wasn't sustainable in the long run. No matter how many days in a row I managed to do the stretching and core exercises, the behavior never became automatic.

The good news is, you get to pick whatever you want your cue to be. It could be waking up, eating lunch, showering, going to the bathroom, getting home from work, whatever. Pick something that happens every single day (or perhaps every week, depending on how often you want to do the desired behavior). Follow the cue with your desired behavior, then the reward. As an example, when I wanted to start meditating, I decided that every day when I walk out of my bedroom (cue), I would go straight to the living room and do my meditation (behavior). After meditating, I would sit down and have coffee with my wife (reward).[42]

The other mistake people tend to make when creating new habit loops is not picking an appropriate reward. You want the reward to have a magnitude in scale with the desired behavior. If it's a relatively easy or quick behavior—like jour-

---

42   You'll notice I left desire out of this loop. It's helpful to understand the desire aspect of the habit loop, especially when trying to modify existing habits, but as you create new habits—and then begin stacking them—it can be easier to omit desire and focus on the cue, behavior, and reward. The desire for your chosen reward will be created naturally over time.

naling for five minutes or cleaning your cat's litter box—the reward can be something small, like having a cup of coffee or putting a gold star on your checklist. If the behavior is more difficult—like two hours of deep work or a weekly extra-long run—you might need something bigger, like an episode of television or a meal from one of your favorite restaurants.

With the right cue and reward, if you repeat the loop enough times, you'll establish the habit.

MAKE IT EASY—START SMALL, THEN STACK

Creating habits takes work. If you try to do too much too quickly, you'll have a harder time establishing the habit. But if you start small, once the habit is in place, it's easy to add to it.

As you begin working to break unproductive habit loops and establish better ones, make it easy on yourself. Remove all the tiny roadblocks that get in the way of your desired behavior. For instance, lay your exercise clothes out the night before so you don't have to search in the morning, or leave the blender out on the counter instead of hiding it in the cupboard so it's easier to make your fruit-and-veggie smoothie. Start small and focus on one behavior at a time, keeping things easily achievable.

Let's say you want to start running for thirty minutes every morning. If you jump right in and try to run thirty minutes every day right away, you're probably going to burn out quickly. But what if you were to start with just ten minutes a day? We can actually break this down even more. You could start simply by putting on your running gear. For a whole week, get up and put on your running clothes, then reward yourself with a cup of coffee or whatever. Then the next week, you can add a step: put on your running gear, walk to the end of your driveway, then come back in and drink your coffee. The next week, another step: put on your running gear, walk to the end of your driveway, keep going around the block, then drink your coffee. And so on, until you're running thirty minutes each morning.

When you're planning it out, it seems like it'll be an eternity before you're actually running every day. That's okay! We're talking about taking a few weeks to build a habit that can last you for decades (many hundreds of weeks) and contribute majorly to your mental and physical health. Is it more important to shave a few weeks off between now and your first "real run" or to improve the chances that you'll be running consistently for the next ten years?

~~~~~

On the timescale of a career or a lifetime, a few weeks of slow start is a small investment with big payoffs. So start small and easy with your habits and build over time.

~~~~~

Once the habit is ingrained, you won't need the reward so directly after the cue. You can then make the desired behavior longer or do habit stacking, where you add other behaviors into the loop. New behaviors can be added to the loop anytime between the initial cue and the final reward—before, between, or after existing habit behaviors. For me, once meditating had become a habit, I stacked my stretching exercises in front of it: walk out of my bedroom (cue); go straight to the living room, stretch, and meditate (behavior); drink coffee with my wife (reward). Then once that, too, had become an ingrained habit, I added in some core exercises. Now, a habit that started with a five-minute guided meditation has turned into a thirty-minute routine, with stretching, core work, and a longer meditation. It would have been a lot harder to establish a thirty-minute routine with three different activities right at the start, but because I added small bits at a time, I was able to build up small successes. These stacked on one another and added up to consistently better mental and physical health.

Stacking Habits

Morning Routine

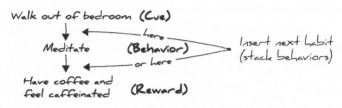

Walk out of bedroom **(Cue)**

Meditate **(Behavior)**

Have coffee and feel caffeinated **(Reward)**

here — *or here* → Insert next habit (stack behaviors)

Adding Stretching

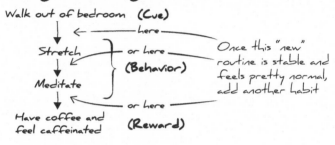

Walk out of bedroom **(Cue)**

Stretch

Meditate **(Behavior)**

Have coffee and feel caffeinated **(Reward)**

here — *or here* — *or here*

Once this "new" routine is stable and feels pretty normal, add another habit

---

Adding Core Exercises

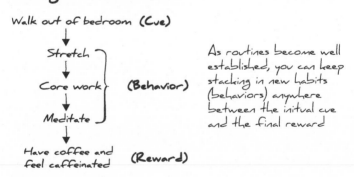

Walk out of bedroom **(Cue)**

Stretch

Core work **(Behavior)**

Meditate

Have coffee and feel caffeinated **(Reward)**

As routines become well established, you can keep stacking in new habits (behaviors) anywhere between the initial cue and the final reward

STICK WITH IT

The final step is to repeat the habit loop until it becomes automatic. The internet and hundreds of self-help books are awash with the idea that if you just do something every day for twenty-one days (or a month, or ninety days, or whatever), it'll be a habit. That's simply not true. First of all, that advice glosses over the fact that a habit is formed by linking a cue and a behavior, not by repetition alone. Additionally, the length of time needed to form (or break) a habit will vary depending on the individual and the behavior. It could take just a couple of weeks, or if you're like me, it might take months for a habit to really sink in. It may take time, but if you keep the loop consistent, eventually it will become ingrained. Your desired behavior will become automatic, such that it feels more natural to do the behavior than not. If something happens that disturbs your routine, you'll feel off.

Maybe you try really hard to stick with it, but you fall out of the behavior before it has a chance to become a habit. What should you do? First, take the pressure off yourself. You're human—these things happen. Then check in and make sure this is a habit you still want to build. If so, it's time to evaluate and see if there's anything you can do to better set yourself up for success. Is your reason motivating enough? Whatever you're using as your reason now, ask yourself "Why?" a couple more times. What's the deepest motivation you can get to? Are you using a good cue? Maybe you decided to use lunch as a cue, but meetings keep popping up immediately after your lunch break so you can't consistently do the behavior you wanted. Then it's time to choose a different cue. Is your desired behavior specific enough? Maybe you decided that every morning, when you first wake up, you're going to exercise. "Exercise" is pretty vague—you still have to decide what specific exercise you're going to do, what you need to wear for that exercise, and where you're going to do the exercise. Pick something specific so that all those decisions are made already. Is your chosen habit realistic, or do you need to scale back? Are you using an appropriate reward? You don't want to get into a mental arms race of constantly escalating rewards, but maybe your chosen reward simply isn't strong enough.

Often, the biggest hurdle isn't doing the behavior, it's getting started. I once set a goal of taking a twenty-minute walk after work before heading home. It helped me clear my head after a stressful or frustrating day, and I enjoyed it. Since the behavior was its own reward, I thought the habit would be easy to build, but I still found myself struggling. On gray, rainy days (a frequency in the Pacific Northwest), I didn't always feel like walking, and sometimes I didn't have time for a full twenty minutes. Instead of skipping my walk on those days, I committed to at least walking around the block, which only takes about three minutes. It is a pretty rare and dramatic rush of an evening when three minutes is more than I can afford for time, and it's a lot easier to find the willpower for a three-minute walk than a twenty-minute one. But in order to take that short walk, I still have to drop my stuff off in my car and put on my rain jacket if needed, just like I would for a longer walk. Since I'm already geared up, once I get moving, that one block almost always turns into a longer walk.

There will likely be days when you feel like you don't have the energy to do your desired behavior, but if you commit to at least *starting*, then worst-case scenario, you're still building the habit of starting the behavior, and best-case scenario, you'll find you actually do have the energy after all.

I also recommend tracking your habits in some way, either in a journal or through an app.[43] This will help give you a big-picture view of your progress. It can also alert you to when you've become inconsistent or fallen out of a habit, which can help you get back into the habit sooner. Many apps gamify the process, using animations and sounds that can make checking off your habits surprisingly satisfying. A lot of apps also use the idea of streaks, which really works for me. The idea of missing a day and seeing my streak drop back down to zero is painful. Avoiding that can often be enough extra motivation to get me to stick with a habit on a tough day. Most apps seem to be focused on daily or weekly habits, so I also use a calendar or some checkboxes in a journal to keep track of my monthly and seasonal routines.

Sticking with the behavior until it becomes a habit can be difficult, but you *can* do it, and the rewards can last a lifetime.

HABITS LEAD TO STEADY, CONSISTENT PROGRESS

Habits are a powerful tool. While bad habits often form without conscious thought, good habits aren't often going to just spring into existence. You need to make an effort to create them. By understanding the cue-behavior-reward loop and starting small, you'll increase your likelihood of success. You can continue building and stacking habits over time.

While bad habits can be frustrating to break, good habits are the key to steady, consistent progress toward achieving your goals and improving your career, life, and well-being. The more things you put on autopilot, the further you'll go, with

---

43   I personally use the Streaks app, but there are many options out there, including free ones.

less effort. Not every action will make a good habit, but every good habit will propel you toward your desired future and leave you more energy and mental capacity for other actions.

Change is hard. If you fall out of a habit, forgive yourself, reset, and reevaluate. But keep at it, and don't give up. It took fifteen years of attempts before I successfully built a habit of stretching and doing core exercises. Today, I'd have to go back through several journals to find the last time I skipped this routine, and it's a habit I hope to continue for the rest of my life.

Turning the steps of your actionable plan into habits will go a long way to keeping you on track to your goals. Challenges may still arise, though. In the next chapter, we'll cover strategies to help you stay committed, even when the going gets tough.

CHAPTER 10

—

STAY ON TRACK WITH COMMITMENT

Great works are performed not by strength, but perseverance.
—SAMUEL JOHNSON

Remember me telling you that I kept deciding to learn how to play guitar, but then never actually did it? I followed all the same advice I give you here in the book. I made an actionable plan. I defined a specific goal—play, from memory, songs my friends and I could recognize and sing or play along to. Then I set mid-level goals I wanted to achieve—specific riffs or songs I wanted to be able to play. Next I broke the steps down until I had something achievable I could turn into a habit: practice twenty minutes a day.

Then I applied what I knew about building habits. I made the behavior easy by buying a cheap guitar stand and keeping my guitar right next to the living room couch. Now, instead of going to the hall closet, retrieving the case, getting the guitar out, moving the case out of the way, and finally sitting down to play, I can literally reach the guitar from the end of the couch. It is as easy to grab the guitar as it is to grab the TV remote. Then I designed a habit loop. I picked a cue (right after the rest of my morning routine) and a reward (coffee).

And guess what? I still didn't learn how to play the guitar. The habit didn't stick. Does this mean all my advice is crap and you should go burn this book? Nope! I was just missing the final step: *commitment*. I've shared tips and strategies to help with deciding and following through on your decisions, but that doesn't mean all of this is easy—just eas*ier*. At the end of the day, you still need to commit and put in the work.

WHY COMMITMENT MATTERS

In the simplest terms, committing makes us more successful. If you don't commit to your goals and your actionable plan, you're probably not going to follow through on them, and you'll never achieve what you want.

Big truly life-changing goals take time to complete, and you need commitment to stay the course.

Interestingly, though, commitment does more than increase our chances of success. It can also increase our happiness. One simple study on this effect looked at satisfaction with a decision, based on whether participants had to commit to the decision.[44] Participants were enrolled in a photography course, and at the completion of the course, they were divided into two groups. Each group got to pick one picture to take home with them. In one group, participants had the option to return that photo in the future and exchange it for another that they would rather have at home instead. In the second group, the choice was binding. They had to commit to the photo they would take home, and there was no option for future exchange.

When asked in advance, the participants predicted that they would be happier if they had an option to exchange their photo. It just makes sense—if you choose a photo and still like it, you're happy, and if you don't like it as much as you thought you would, you can exchange it. Yet when surveyed some time later, people who did not have the option to exchange their photo were happier about their choice than the people who did.

It turns out that, when we commit to something, our brain works to reinforce that commitment by looking for the reasons we made a good choice. If we think about being bound by the choice, it may make us uncomfortable. But mostly, since we can't change the commitment, our brain makes the best of it, looking for information that reinforces our decision, which makes us happier about the choice. In contrast, if we haven't made a binding decision, our brain instead looks for reasons we might want to change or upgrade our choice. Naturally, that leads to us questioning our choice more and being less happy with it.

---

44   D. T. Gilbert and J. E. J. Ebert, "Decisions and Revisions: The Affective Forecasting of Changeable
       Outcomes," *Journal of Personality and Social Psychology* 82, no. 4 (2002): 503–14.

You might be thinking, "Wait, how is this different from the sunk cost fallacy? Isn't it a bad thing to stick to something because you feel like you have to?" The difference is that with the sunk cost fallacy, you're looking backward at the investment you've already made. With commitment, you're looking forward to the future you're building. Remember that persistence *is* useful. It only ceases to be useful when what we're persisting toward isn't what we want.

WHY WE STRUGGLE WITH COMMITMENT

If commitment is so great, why is it so hard? We often fall into a fixed mindset when it comes to commitment. "I'm just bad at commitment," we think. "I don't have the discipline for it." There are a lot of reasons we struggle with commitment, but "being bad at commitment" isn't one of them.

One of the biggest reasons we don't commit is a failure to plan, or a failure to plan effectively. We say we want to do something, but we don't make a plan for *how*, so of course we don't do it. Or we do make a plan, but it's too vague, so we can't act on it and don't hold ourselves to it.

The next big reason is that we hit bumps in the road. When you first make a goal and plan, you're probably excited and raring to go. You're not thinking about the roadblocks you're going to hit. You're thinking about your ideal future—everything you want. So then when you do hit roadblocks, you're caught off guard and discouraged. This can derail you, especially if you're thinking with a fixed mindset. "Well, this didn't work out," you may think. "Guess I can't do it." You may then abandon your goal entirely.

So while the traditional advice is that you should envision your success, you shouldn't *just* envision your success. You do want to believe in your success, but to make that success more likely, you're actually better off envisioning the roadblocks and the ways you may fail or hit setbacks. The benefits of deliberately considering your obstacles and ways you might fail have been demonstrated in studies across many realms of life: general goal pursuit, weight loss, quitting smoking, work–life balance, creative endeavors, and more.[45] Of course, no matter how much you plan and prepare for roadblocks, you can't predict the future. You will still face some challenges you didn't anticipate, so you will need to draw on your growth mindset at those times.

Finally, the last big reason we struggle with commitment is our cognitive biases—specifically time discounting and exponential growth bias. Just as our biases make it difficult to follow through on our decisions, they also make it difficult for us to stay committed.

Following the advice in previous chapters *will* help you better commit to your goals, but if you're still struggling, no worries. There are additional strategies you can use to help you stay committed.

---

45 A. Kappes and G. Oettingen, "The Emergence of Goal Pursuit: Mental Contrasting Connects Future and Reality," *Journal of Experimental Social Psychology* 54 (2014): 25–39; G. Oettingen and T. A. Wadden, "Expectation, Fantasy, and Weight Loss: Is the Impact of Positive Thinking Always Positive?," *Cognitive Therapy and Research* 15 (1991): 167–75; Gabriele Oettingen, Doris Mayer, and Jennifer Thorpe, "Self-Regulation of Commitment to Reduce Cigarette Consumption: Mental Contrasting of Future with Reality," *Psychology & Health* 25, no. 8 (2010): 961–77; G. Oettingen, D. Mayer, and B. Brinkmann, "Mental Contrasting of Future and Reality: Managing the Demands of Everyday Life in Health Care Professionals," *Journal of Personnel Psychology* 9 (2010): 138–44; G. Oettingen, M. K. Marquardt, and P. M. Gollwitzer, "Mental Contrasting Turns Positive Feedback on Creative Potential into Successful Performance," *Journal of Experimental Social Psychology* 48 (2012): 990–96.

COMMIT CLEARLY AND PUBLICLY

Have you ever signed up for a race in order to "force yourself" to train for it? If you're married, did you perform the ceremony privately or in front of a number of guests (witnesses)? Have you ever agreed to do something you weren't quite ready for, knowing that simply agreeing to it would give you the push you needed to do the work? Clear, explicit commitments help us stick to our goals, and public commitments are even stronger than promises we make to ourselves.

The simple first step to this is to make a clear commitment to yourself. Multiple studies show that writing down a commitment increases success much more than simply thinking it to yourself.[46] So write down a commitment to one of your goals: "I will..." Then keep that written commitment someplace where you'll see it regularly.

Make the commitment something you have full control over. If you're searching for a job, for example, don't make your commitment "I will get a new job within one month," because that depends on a lot of factors you can't control. It's not fair to you to make commitments you might not be able to keep, despite your best efforts. Instead, you could make the commitment. "I will apply to at least three new positions every week."

A written commitment is a good start, but in general, we're

---

46   Gail Matthews, "The Impact of Commitment, Accountability, and Written Goals on Goal Achievement," Psychology | Faculty Presentations 3 (2007): https://scholar.dominican.edu/psychology-faculty-conference-presentations/3; G. Oettingen, H.-j. Pak, and K. Schnetter, "Self-Regulation of Goal-Setting: Turning Free Fantasies about the Future into Binding Goals," *Journal of Personality and Social Psychology* 80, no. 5 (2001): 736–53; Akira Miyake, Lauren E. Kost-Smith, Noah D. Finkelstein, Steven J. Pollock, Geoffrey L. Cohen, and Tiffany A. Ito, "Reducing the Gender Achievement Gap in College Science: A Classroom Study of Values Affirmation," *Science* 330, no. 6008 (2010): 1234–37.

better at keeping public and interpersonal commitments than personal ones. We tell our boss we'll finish a task by the end of the week, and we do. We tell our friends we'll meet them at a certain day and time, and we do. We feel pressure to keep these commitments because if we don't, we risk disappointing or angering the other party and perhaps damaging the relationship. But if the commitment is only to yourself, the only person you're going to disappoint or anger is you, and you can always choose to let yourself off the hook.

Ultimately, while we're often told that we shouldn't care what other people think of us, we're social creatures. *Of course* we care what other people think of us—and we can use that to our benefit. Fear of the possible social sanction if we fail to live up to our promises can be powerfully motivating. For example, most of us would be embarrassed if we posted on social media that we were going to volunteer at the food bank on Thanksgiving and then failed to do so.

There are many ways you can make your commitment public, such as posting about it on social media or sharing it with family and friends. With my guitar example, I made a commitment to practice twenty minutes a day for ninety days straight. I wrote it down and told my family and a few friends I was committing to this goal. This was no joke, because my kids have no hesitation about calling me out on stuff like this. It became payback for all the times I've told *them* to practice their musical instruments.

Is it stressful to put your commitment out in the open like this? It can be, and that's kind of the point. The reason it's scary to make commitments this way is because we're worried about what will happen if we don't keep the commitment.

That fear and worry make us feel more obligated to follow through, even in the face of challenges.

USE CARROTS AND STICKS

Public commitment works because you're essentially putting your social reputation at stake—but sometimes that's not enough. In that case, you can raise the stakes even higher by using carrots (rewards) and sticks (punishments).

~~~

Some days, you simply won't have the motivation to work toward your goals. Having something specific at stake can give you the push you need to keep moving forward.

~~~

We already discussed in the previous chapter the ways that little, immediate rewards can help us build habits. A similar strategy, using bigger rewards connected to specific goals, can help with motivation in the longer term. Having a big reward to look forward to can help keep you committed even on the days when the little reward of your habit loop doesn't seem enough.

Let's say you want to improve your fitness, and your specific goal is to run a half marathon. You've been trying to train, but haven't managed to run consistently enough to get beyond the local 5k fun run. Now let's say you've also been considering taking a Hawaii vacation. You've wanted to go for years, and you can finally afford it. You can use the vacation as a carrot: "I will take that Hawaii vacation in September, but only if I complete a half marathon by the end of June." A Hawaii vacation is a big reward. On a dark and rainy April morning, when the promise of your post-run blueberry muffin just isn't enough to get you out the door, the thought of your Hawaii vacation will help you stick to your training plan.

The reward doesn't have to be as big as a vacation. It just has to be something you actually want and are willing to put at stake, because if you *don't* meet your goal, you can't give yourself the reward—that would completely defeat the purpose. There are lots of things you could choose as a reward. Material items—from something small like a new book to something bigger like a gaming console—can be good rewards because they are easy to visualize. Travel is often a big reward for many of us, and time can also work. What if you promised yourself a weekday off to chill at home with no projects to do and nobody else around, but only once you've met your savings goal for three months in a row?

With my guitar practice, I wanted an inexpensive guitar I could keep in my car or my office so that I could practice and pass the time with it during long periods (sometimes hours) when I have to be near the hospital but have nothing specific to do. So I promised myself that if I could maintain my daily practice with zero missed days for ninety days, I would buy myself a second guitar.

You can also add in a negative consequence for failing to meet your goal. Remember way back in Chapter 2 when we talked about how we're more afraid of losing what we have than we are excited about what we might gain? While that psychological tendency can do a lot of damage in some settings, we can use it to our advantage in motivating ourselves. If we fail to meet our goal, we can carry out a punishment, metaphorically whacking ourselves with a stick.

For guitar practice, I put $100 on the line. I got a nice, crisp $100 bill from the bank and deducted it from my monthly personal spending budget. Then I printed out a calendar for the next ninety days, and I paper-clipped the $100 bill to the first day. Each day I practiced guitar, I could move the bill to the next day. If I failed to practice, I would have to burn the bill. Since the money had been subtracted from my budget, that would mean losing out on the things I would normally spend the money on—a gadget, a massage, a new journal, or a lunch out on a busy day. When I told my family my plan, they thought I was crazy. But I wasn't crazy; I was *committed*.

You don't have to commit to literally burning money for this to work. It could be giving up something else you value—maybe you don't get to watch TV or you have to go without your favorite food for a certain amount of time. Another popular strategy is donating money to something you dislike, like the archrivals of your favorite sports team or a political cause you disagree with. I considered trying this strategy but couldn't find the right balance. I'm not enough of a sports fan to really feel bad about donating to my favorite team's rival, and I would feel *too* bad donating to political causes I disagree with, so much so that I don't believe I'd actually follow through with it. I'd rather burn several $100 bills for no reason at all than donate them to causes I see as harmful. The point is, for this technique to work, you have to care about what's at stake, and you also have to be willing to follow through with the punishment if you fail to meet your commitment.

We're all animals who respond to rewards and threats. By creating our own carrot-and-stick system, we can give ourselves a couple of big pushes toward our goals. How will you reward yourself for achieving your big goals? How about smaller rewards for the steps along the way? Is there something you can put at stake to help you follow through?

REMEMBER YOUR REASON AND ENVISION YOUR FUTURE SELF

Rewards and punishments can be very motivating, but it's important that they don't take over as our reason for pursuing a goal. It's easy for this to happen because the rewards and punishments tend to be very concrete, more immediate, and much easier to visualize and anticipate than our big reason for the goal. Just compare "Hawaii vacation" to "improved fitness" or "not having to burn $100" to "being able to play guitar with friends." If we're not careful, we start to think getting the reward or avoiding the punishment is the reason— we're exercising so we can go to Hawaii (rather than for our fitness), or we're practicing guitar so we don't have to burn money (rather than for our future happiness). This effect seems to be most pronounced with financial rewards but can occur with any type of incentive.

If you lose sight of your real reason for pursuing a goal, your motivation will fade, as will your ability to overcome challenges.

While your short-term rewards and punishments may be easier to picture, they don't have the same force as your big, outward-focused reason does. So make sure you remember your real reason. One simple strategy to do this is to write it down, just like with your commitment, and put it somewhere you can easily review it. If you're trying to quit smoking, for instance, maybe you have a note that says, "I'm quitting smoking because my kids' health is more important to me. I don't want to expose them to the smoke or model an unhealthy habit." You can then put the note where you'll see it when you're tempted to smoke, like with your lighter. It's a cheap and easy—but powerful—tool to help stay on track.

Envisioning your future self is another way you can really cement your reason. When I don't feel like practicing guitar, I think about sixty-year-old Fred. How will he feel about still not being able to play guitar, versus being twenty years into practicing and playing consistently? Future Fred definitely wants to be sitting on the porch playing classic rock songs with his friends rather than in the living room relearning the C major scale.

Remembering your reason and envisioning the future you want will help motivate you to take consistent action now. I've brought up both of these strategies a couple of times now, and it's because they're not one-and-done activities. They're things you should do anytime you're lacking motivation.

SOLICIT EXTERNAL SUPPORT

These are your goals, and it's your commitment to reach them, but you don't have to do it all alone. Ask for help! External support greatly increases our chances of success at reaching our goals, and that support can come in many ways.

One option is to hire a coach or teacher. Nowadays, you can find a coach for just about anything, and they can not only provide helpful advice, but also help hold you accountable. Having a piano lesson every Friday, for instance, increases the odds that you'll practice during the week, because you know that your teacher has expectations about your improvement in between lessons.

You could also join a group that shares your same goal and meets regularly, like a workout group, book club, or professional development organization. Even if the group isn't made up of natural cheerleaders, just the fact that you know the other group members will be there and they expect you to be there too increases the odds of you showing up and actually doing the work. Even joining a group on social media can be beneficial. Seeing others working toward a similar goal can be motivating, and once you're there, the other members will also be able to share their tips and relevant subject knowledge. As a side benefit, by joining the group, you are further advertising your commitment and making it public.

It doesn't have to be a group, either—it could just be a single friend pursuing the same goal. Having a workout buddy, for example, increases your commitment because on your low-motivation days, your buddy will still be going to the gym and expecting you to join them. Quitting smoking with a friend can give you someone to check in with. You can share stories about the toughest times and hold each other accountable if you slip up and have a smoke.

You can even get great social support from someone who isn't interested in the same goal as you. Have a friend trying to get fit for a half marathon while you're trying to write a book? Make a deal with one another: you'll text your friend every day after finishing at least two writing sessions, and your friend will text after finishing their training for the day. If either of you hasn't texted by 7:00 p.m., the other will call to check in.

Not all goals lend themselves well to a buddy system or a group, but you can still benefit from social support in almost any scenario. Trying to save up to buy a house? Do you know anyone who has done that before? Give them a call and ask for advice—ask about strategies that helped them, things they would have done differently, or things they wish they'd known ahead of time. Most people like sharing their experiences. With a few questions and an open mind, you can learn a lot.

Sometimes all you need is a commitment referee—someone who knows about your goal and will hold you accountable. I turned my entire family into commitment referees for my guitar practice goal. They would call me out when I didn't practice, and as much as they teased me about my $100 bill idea at first, they're the ones who would've grabbed the lighter and set it aflame if I missed a practice. You could also enlist friends or colleagues for this role. In choosing a commitment referee, just make sure that (1) they don't have anything to gain by you failing (you don't want them deliberately undermining you!), and (2) they're willing to follow through and enforce any consequences you've set for yourself—they actually will mail your check to the rival college booster club or light up that $100 bill while you watch. If you don't have someone who would make a good commitment referee, you can outsource this duty with a web service or app.[47]

We all need help and support sometimes.

If you try to do it all alone, you might end up sabotaging yourself, especially when you hit bumps in the road. I sometimes wonder what would've happened if, during my surgery residency, I didn't have my wife to help remind me of my reason for going into surgery in the first place. At the very least, I would've continued feeling unmotivated and disengaged. Or I might've decided to switch to radiology, and today, I probably wouldn't be as happy. Your goals are important to your future happiness and well-being. So use all the resources available to you in order to hold your commitment.

---

47 One option is stickK. StickK tracks results, and using this method, they have helped tens of thousands of people hit financial goals, quit smoking, reach fitness goals, and achieve many other goals defined by the individual users.

KEEPING TRACTION AND AVOIDING DISTRACTION

EXERCISE: TIME MANAGEMENT MATRIX

In his book *Indistractable*, researcher Nir Eyal talks about *traction* and *distraction*. *Traction*, as he defines it, is anything that moves you toward your goal, while *distraction* is anything that does not. As you work toward your goals, you're undoubtedly going to face interruptions—extra responsibilities at work, a TV show that sucks you in, new opportunities, a family crisis. You only have so much time each day, and with so many things competing for your time and attention, it's easy to get pulled off track. So periodically, you should take an inventory of how you spend your time, with the goal of maximizing traction activities and minimizing distraction.

However, some distractions, even if they don't move us toward our goal, are important and valuable. For instance, if one of my kids gets injured, that's going to take priority over practicing guitar. So it's not as easy as "simply" eliminating all distraction. How, then, can you make sure you're using your time effectively, keeping traction while avoiding too much distraction? You can use a *time management matrix*, an exercise popularized by productivity expert Stephen Covey.

A time management matrix is a two-by-two grid, with four quadrants into which we can sort our activities based on urgency and importance. You don't have to graph this out every time for the exercise to be useful; it's about having a framework to mentally sort and prioritize your activities.

Time Management Matrix

	Urgent	Not Urgent
Important	**1 Necessity** (Urgent and important) 🔥 Do it now: • Crises • Important tight deadlines • Pressing problems	**2 Productivity** (Important, not urgent) ⊕ Schedule it and focus: • Strategy, planning • Prevention • Building skills, capabilities, relationships
Not Important	**3 Distraction** (Not important but seemingly urgent) 🔔 Delegate or push back: • Interruptions • Other people's priorities • Nonproductive emails, calls, meetings	**4 Waste** (Not important and not urgent) 🗑 Discard or push back: • Interruptions • Trivial tasks/busy work • Mindless scrolling

Quadrant 1: High Urgency, High Importance

Quadrant 1 is made up of things we have to deal with right away—like an injured child, a network outage across our online business, something literally on fire (that isn't supposed to be), major customer complaints, or failure of the hard drive with your thesis data on it. We have to spend time in this quadrant when these things come up, but we would be more productive and more successful if we could prevent or avoid these situations, rather than repeatedly getting caught up in them. So if you have a lot of things in this category, it could be a sign that you need to spend more time planning to avoid distraction.

Quadrant 2: Low Urgency, High Importance

Quadrant 2 is where we should try to spend most of our time—things that are of great importance, but not (yet) urgent. These are things that need to be planned for, and planning itself goes in this category. This category includes things like saving money, exercise, self-care, and goal setting and goal pursuit. This is where we spend our time when we are at our best, and it's where we get the most traction.

Quadrant 3: High Urgency, Low Importance

Quadrant 3 is a trap. It's stuff that sucks us in because it is presented as or seems urgent but isn't actually important. This category includes things like other people's problems that they want to be our problems or phone calls, text messages, and any other alerts designed to give us a sense of urgency but rarely signifying anything of significant value to us. These things can be major distractions, and we should try to minimize or eliminate them.

Quadrant 4: Low Urgency, Low Importance

Quadrant 4 is mostly wasted time and energy. It includes things like scrolling social media mindlessly, watching TV you're not interested in and get nothing out of, and taking an extra twenty minutes to get dressed in the morning because you can't decide between the jeggings in Savoy blue or Celtic blue. These are largely distractions, and there aren't many that you should deliberately choose to keep in your life. There is a caveat here, though. Depending on the intent of the activity, some seemingly Quadrant 4 activities can actually be classified in Quadrant 1 or Quadrant 2. For example, playing Tetris mindlessly for an hour when you should be sleeping, or exercising, or spending time with people you care about? That's Quadrant 4. But playing Tetris to decrease your risk of PTSD and flashbacks after exposure to significant trauma (yes, this is a real thing that works[48])? That's important and time-sensitive, so it's Quadrant 1. Similarly, social

---

48   Iyadurai et al., "Preventing Intrusive Memories after Trauma via a Brief Intervention Involving Tetris Computer Game Play in the Emergency Department: A Proof-Of-Concept Randomized Controlled Trial," *Molecular Psychology* 23 (2018): 674–82; Kessler et al., "Reducing Intrusive Memories of Trauma Using a Visuospatial Interference Intervention with Inpatients with Posttraumatic Stress Disorder (PTSD)," *Journal of Consulting and Clinical Psychology* 86, no. 12 (2018): 1076.

media could be moved to Quadrant 2 if you're using it to stay in contact with people you care about or to manage your digital presence.

So, which quadrants are you spending most of your time in? What can you do to reprioritize and start spending more of your time in Quadrant 2, working on your goals? As new things come up, consider where they fit to help decide how (or even if) to deal with them.

NO ROAD IS PERFECTLY SMOOTH, BUT COMMITMENT WILL SEE YOU THROUGH

Few things in life are certain, with the exception that you are going to face challenges, unexpected interruptions, and distractions. That's just part of life. But no matter what road-blocks you hit, if you're committed to your goal and your plan, you'll almost always be able to move past the challenges.

You are capable of doing hard things, as long as you stay committed. Commitment isn't something that just happens; it's something you build. There are lots of strategies for increasing it, and the more you use, the better. So make a public commitment, establish incentives and put something at stake, remember your reason, and solicit external support.

Now that you have some specific tips to help with day-to-day commitment, in the final chapter, we'll discuss the big-picture strategies to make long-term progress toward your goals.

CHAPTER 11

MAKE LONG-TERM PROGRESS: KEEP PRACTICING AND LEARNING

Practice makes the master.
—PATRICK ROTHFUSS, *THE NAME OF THE WIND*

Periodically at my hospital, my partners and I get together for something called a morbidity and mortality (M&M) conference. It's an opportunity for us to review and analyze any cases that resulted in a bad outcome. We work to determine whether the bad outcome was preventable or simply due to chance, with the goal of learning from the experience and better preventing similar bad outcomes in the future.

For each bad outcome, we go through every step of the patient's care in a systematic way. We start at the very beginning. The surgeon involved in the case will explain, "This is how the patient came to me, and this is what I knew at the time." The rest of us don't know the details of the outcome or the decisions made along the way. We can provide some objectivity, sharing what decisions we would have made and what actions we would have taken in that same situation.

First we'll look at the diagnosis: Was there more the surgeon should have done to find out what was wrong? Did they get the diagnosis right?

Let's say the diagnosis was right. Then we'll look at the treatment plan. Based on the diagnosis, do the rest of us agree with the chosen treatment plan? Does the available science agree with the chosen treatment plan? Should the surgeon have done more? Less? Something different?

If the plan was a reasonable one to follow, then should the surgeon have executed it differently? Should they have used a different surgical technique? Did the surgeon make any mistakes during the procedure?

If we don't identify any execution mistakes, it looks like the bad outcome was just bad luck. Perhaps this operation has an 11 percent chance of resulting in an infection, even when the surgeon does everything right. So now we ask, is there anything we can do to drive that number down? Are there ways we could further mitigate that risk or catch such infections earlier?

At any point in this analysis process, we might discover mistakes or opportunities for improvement. We then take that information and apply it to future cases, constantly refining the level of care we provide.

While my description here is fairly clinical, it can be an incredibly difficult process emotionally. Like many doctors, I went into medicine to help people. Though I know it's impossible to achieve a good outcome 100 percent of the time, that doesn't stop me from *wanting* a good outcome in every single case. When something goes wrong, even if it's due to chance, I feel terrible. Then, sharing that bad outcome with my colleagues, I often feel a bit of shame. It's easy to fall down a rabbit hole of "If I'd only known _____" or "If I'd only done _____."

On some level, I'm sure you've experienced similar feelings of shame when dealing with failures or mistakes, but this is all part of the process of learning and growing. If surgeons had spent the last hundred years trying to cover up their mistakes instead of learning from them, we would have missed out on a lot of progress. With M&M conferences, constant learning is built into the surgical process. As a surgeon, you participate in these conferences from the very first week of your training through the end of your career. The process is so normalized that it can actually be therapeutic. By openly discussing bad outcomes and mistakes, we can recognize that as doctors we're still human, and we can release the shame that surrounds our failure to be perfect. Most importantly, by getting feedback from one another and learning from our own and each other's mistakes and bad outcomes, we become better at what we do.

~~~~~

Nobody's perfect, and none of us ever will be. Facing mistakes and failure can be difficult, but it's more important to learn than to defend ourselves.

~~~~~

In this final chapter, we'll pull together some previously discussed concepts and discuss how you can set yourself up for long-term success. You can become a focused, lifelong learner, able to face whatever challenges life throws your way.

REMEMBER YOUR GROWTH MINDSET: GET GRITTY

We often revere the "naturals" in life, whether it's in sports, business, academics, entertainment, or whatever. We like to hold up our stars and claim they were "born with it" or "destined for greatness." But we also have lots of sayings like "Rome wasn't built in a day" and "If at first you don't succeed, try, try again." Why do we try to have it both ways? Why do we so often look up to our heroes and say they are lucky to have such talent, but look down to those less successful than ourselves and tell them they could be just like us, if only they worked harder?

The answer is easy and obvious, but not nice: thinking this way makes us feel better about ourselves. If we convince ourselves that other people's success is a result of luck and talent, we don't have to feel bad in comparison. And if we convince ourselves that our own success is due strictly to hard work, we can feel great about that too.

As an example, most people would agree that Will Smith has had a resoundingly successful professional life. He has released nine studio albums and has four Grammy Awards as a hip-hop artist. He starred in a television sitcom that ran for six years, he's been nominated for five Golden Globes and two Academy Awards for his roles in film, and his total filmography has grossed over $7.5 billion. If I believe that Will Smith was born with talent and I wasn't, I don't have to feel bad about not practicing my acting. I simply wasn't destined to be a star.

But if I think, "Will Smith deserves what he's got because, damn, he has worked harder than 99 percent of people in show business," then I have to admit that maybe my own failure to become a successful actor is because I didn't practice enough. Maybe if I'd spent thousands of hours practicing, and auditioning, and going back even if I didn't get the part, and accepting small roles as opportunities to hone my craft... Okay, maybe I still wouldn't be as accomplished an actor as Will Smith. But I'd certainly be a lot more accomplished of an actor than I am now (my last starring role was in a fourth-grade school play). And without having put in a whole lifetime of hard work, I will never know how accomplished I could have been.

Does this mean everyone has the capability to become Will Smith, Mozart, *and* Bobby Fischer, depending on whatever they decide to put their effort into? Probably not. We each have a range of skills we might develop in any one area or pursuit. We stay at the bottom of that range if we never try and never practice. We move up that range with experience, deliberate practice, and coaching (active mentoring). The following graph shows what I mean. Your level of achievement will march up at a slope determined by talent and effort, eventually topping out or plateauing when you reach your personal potential, or you stop trying.

Achievement vs Time Graph

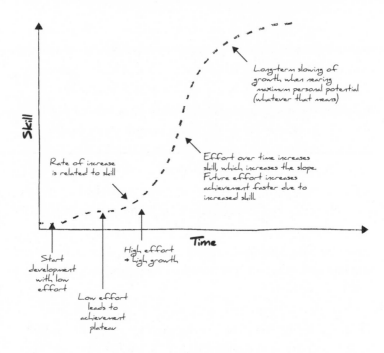

Skill

Long-term slowing of growth when nearing maximum personal potential (whatever that means)

Effort over time increases skill, which increases the slope. Future effort increases achievement faster due to increased skill.

Rate of increase is related to skill

Time

High effort → high growth

Start development with low effort

Low effort leads to achievement plateau

So what does all of this mean? It means that even after reading this book, you're not going to be a natural at decision-making. Whatever your big goals are, you're not going to be a natural at those either. But you *can* get a whole lot better than you are today, if you get gritty.

Grit, as Dr. Angela Duckworth defines it, is a combination of passion and perseverance in pursuit of long-term goals. In her book *Grit*, Duckworth summarizes decades of research looking at achievement in the face of challenges. She acknowledges that there are several factors in achievement, but they are all modified by effort. As she puts it, "Effort counts twice."[49] The amount of skill you develop is a product of "talent" or "natural potential" multiplied by the effort you put in. Your achievement will be a product of the amount of skill you have and the amount of effort you put in. For the math nerds:

Skill = [Potential] × [Effort]

Achievement = [Skill] × [Effort] = [Potential] × [Effort]^2

In other words, effort, potential, and effort some more.

Tim Urban (the TED speaker and *Wait But Why* author, not the American Idol contestant), treats this same concept a slightly different way:

Progress = Pace × Persistence

That is, how far you get will depend on how fast you're going and how long you stick with it. And, of course, your pace depends on your ability and your effort. So, effort, potential, and persistence—or grit.

So, how do you get gritty? You need passion and perseverance, which build on each other. Passion is what will give you the drive and motivation to persevere over the long-term. And as we discussed earlier, passion is often created, not found. Persevering—sticking with something through challenges—may be just the thing that helps you build your passion.

---

49   Angela Duckworth, "Effort Counts Twice," chap. 3 in *Grit: The Power of Passion and Perseverance* (New York: Scribner, 2016).

Something that can help you get this process going is taking advantage of the competence–confidence loop. Doubting your ability to achieve your goals can be a big barrier. It's hard to be gritty if you don't believe that you're capable of improving. Fortunately, if you have even a tiny bit of either confidence or competence, you can use it to build the other. You can even draw on confidence and competence from other areas of your life.

The Competence-Confidence Loop

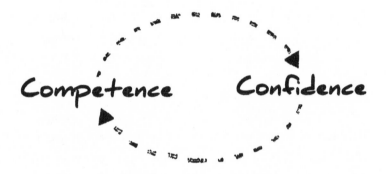

When I first started playing guitar, I had almost no competence, but I figured if I could do surgery (something that requires precise control of your hands), I could learn the mechanical skills needed to play guitar, like making chords and plucking strings (things that require precise control of your hands). That confidence in my ability to learn helped me persevere in practicing, which led to greater competence. Then, as I practiced, I was able to draw on my increasing competence to further grow my confidence. You can start this loop with either confidence or competence, no matter how small. For instance, when I sat around plucking the strings, I could recognize that some of the noises I made were more appealing than others. That's a small but important competence in making music, and the more I played, the more I could distinguish what sounded good from what didn't. I could latch on to that to give me more confidence in my ability to learn.

With the competence–confidence loop, you can better persevere as you build your passion. And while that is happening, you can always also be passionate about your future, about securing happiness and well-being for yourself. It's going to be a long ride to achieving your biggest goals, so buckle in and get gritty.

DO LESS, THEN OBSESS

Do you remember the Chapter 5 story about Warren Buffett and his pilot, and the exercise of choosing just five goals? That concept of focus is critical. You could be incredibly gritty, but if you spread your time and energy out over too many things, you'll struggle to advance in any one area as much as you could.

Behavioral science research supports this idea. One simple example involves saving money.[50] When people were asked to list their financial priorities explicitly and measure how much they saved toward their goals over six months, they saved more than those who had not explicitly thought about their priorities. But people who were asked to pick a single goal from that list to focus on? They saved significantly more than those who tried to work toward all their goals at the

---

50   Dilip Soman and Min Zhao, "The Fewer the Better: Number of Goals and Savings Behavior," *Journal of Marketing Research* 48, no. 6 (2011): 944–57.

same time. In fact, they saved more for their one goal than the *total* the others saved for all their goals combined.

Opportunity cost has a role here. You only have so much time and energy. You can't do *everything*. The time and energy you spend on low-priority activities is time and energy you can't spend on your high-priority activities. What's more, when your priorities are divided, your attention is divided. And when your attention is divided, it takes a bit of effort to decide what to focus on at any given moment. It also takes a bit of effort to switch from one priority to another. That is two bits of effort that aren't directed toward achieving *any* of your goals. Sometimes those are small bits, sometimes large, but in any case, they actively take away from your ability to progress toward your top priorities.

So what should we do? In his book *Great at Work*, Morten Hansen summarizes years of research from many studies on top performers across all types of professional endeavors, at all levels of different companies.[51] Among their findings, the single factor with the biggest impact and the best ability to predict excellence is what he and his team came to call "Do less, then obsess."

There are two steps here. The first is to do less. This doesn't mean slacking off or working less. It means focusing your attention on a small number of top priorities. That was the point of the 5/25 exercise in Chapter 5. Be careful and methodical about picking your top priorities, but once you do, you need to focus on them and only them. Don't just reprioritize. Actually get rid of the other goals and projects

---

51   Hansen, *Great at Work*.

that distract you from your top priorities. This might mean quitting some activities, delegating work to someone else, or having a conversation with your boss about adjusting your workload so that you can give your best and really excel at the top priorities.

The second step is to obsess. Don't just narrow your list of projects and half-ass the few that are left. Take all the time and energy you used to spend working on other projects, and pour it into your new focus. Get nerdy with it. Get passionate about it. Foster curiosity and challenge yourself. You have the time and energy to spare now, and these top priorities are all you've got. Give them everything!

Several other authors and researchers, including Angela Duckworth, agree with the idea that you should limit your number of top-level goals to improve your chances of success. In their book *Think Small*, Owain Service and Rory Gallagher actually suggest that you pick a single goal to focus on.[52]

Life is usually a bit too complicated to allow for just one goal overall, so my advice, and what I am finding is both realistic and practical in my life, is to pick a single goal in each realm of your life. The pure advice to pick just one goal would have me choose to either save for my kids' college educations *or* increase my biking mileage month over month, but not both. Now, a cognitive scientist may tell me that even these fairly unrelated goals do compete with each other for space in my mind, but in a practical sense, they can coexist. In fact, to increase my well-being overall, they *must* coexist. I need to pursue a financial goal in the same time period I work on a

---

52   Owain Service and Rory Gallagher, *Think Small: The Surprisingly Simple Ways to Reach Big Goals* (London: Michael O'Mara, 2017).

fitness goal. Along the way I have an educational goal (learn to play guitar), a career goal (maintain above-average surgical volume with below-average complication rates), and a personal goal (publish this book).

These goals *do* compete with each other. I could do more surgery and more quality improvement at the hospital if I didn't do anything else in my life, I could write more if I didn't practice the guitar, I could bike more if I didn't write, and on and on. If I picked just one of these things, I would make progress faster and ultimately go further in it. But I don't think I would be better off in a year, or in five years, or at the end of my life.

The point is that focus matters, but the real world is complex, and our lives in it are multifaceted. So don't be afraid to have more than one goal. But do try to limit yourself to one major goal per major area of your life, and try to pick goals that compete with one another as little as possible. Remember that the *ultimate* goal here is long-term well-being, which requires growth in many realms. So, over time, pick a financial goal. Pick a health or fitness goal. Pick a professional goal. Pick an education or personal development goal. As you identify each of them, focus your energy and start obsessing healthily.

USE THE LEARNING LOOP

So you're building your grit, and you've narrowed your focus. Now how can you make sure you're working and practicing in a way that's effective and leads toward your goals? You've probably heard of the 10,000 hours rule, which suggests it takes 10,000 hours of practice to become an expert in something. You may also have heard that this isn't exactly accurate. Anders Ericsson, whose research helped form the foundation of the "rule," has said that the 10,000 hours rule is an oversimplification and misunderstanding of his and his colleagues' research. For those 10,000 hours to lead to mastery, they must be spent in *deliberate, focused, and goal-oriented practice.*

One of the best ways to ensure you're doing the kind of practice that will lead to mastery is to use what Morten Hansen calls the *learning loop*. I've also heard it called the engineering method.

The basic method is this: Do something. Assess the results. Get feedback on the gap between the desired and actual results. Modify the original activity/plan. (Re)do the thing. Assess the results. Get feedback. Modify. Redo. Assess. Get feedback. And so on and so on.

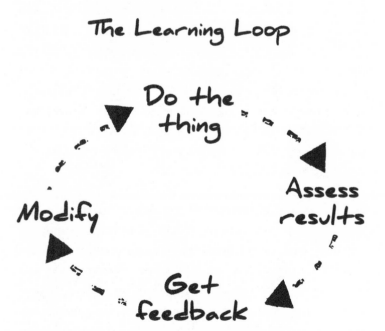

The Learning Loop

Do the thing

Assess results

Get feedback

Modify

Here's an example of what it would like for learning a tennis serve:

- Do: Serve the ball.
- Assess: The serve was long.
- Get feedback: Your coach tells you that you hit the ball too high/too early, or you review your video and see this was the case.
- Modify: Wait a little longer, so your toss can come down further before you strike the ball.
- (Re)do: Serve the ball, with a little delay when you swing compared to last time.
- Assess...

This learning loop works because it makes us focus on what we can *change* to get better. Sometimes we fall into a trap of practicing something over and over but doing it the same way every time, so that all we're doing is ingraining bad habits, not improving. Or we make changes but don't assess the impacts of the change, so we don't know if it actually helped or not. Or maybe we get feedback, but it's not super specific, so we struggle to figure out what we can modify the next time we try the activity. By consciously using the learning loop, we can overcome these issues and make sure we're getting the most out of our practice.

You can consciously enter the learning loop at any stage. When you get a new job, you explore your new commute by going to work on the first day. Having done the commute, you can assess how long it took and how pleasant it was, and move on with the loop from there. If you've been at your current work location for a while, you're already doing your commute and maybe haven't thought about it in a while. You could consciously decide to make a new assessment, timing it and counting the stoplights to see if you can figure out a quicker way. Or maybe you start (re)learning about it when you get some feedback—a coworker moved to your neighborhood and tells you the route they take, and it sounds like it's a lot prettier and no longer than your current habitual drive. Or, as has actually been studied when the London Underground strikes forced thousands of people to modify their commutes,[53] external circumstances (like a strike or construction) may force you to modify your commute. Only after this has happened do you realize that, when you assess the forced modification, it's actually better than the route you had been using for years.

<hr>

Ongoing learning is a cycle, so wherever you choose (or get forced) to enter the loop—do, assess, get feedback, modify—the process still works.

<hr>

You can apply the learning loop to any activity—even something as broad as "decision-making." Of course, the more complicated the activity is, the more complex this process gets. With decision-making, for instance, you're not going to be able to loop through sixty decisions in an hour with time for mentoring and reflection on how each one went. You might not see all the impacts of those decisions for months

---

53 Shaun Larcom, Ferdinand Rauch, and Tim Willems, "The Benefits of Forced Experimentation: Striking Evidence from the London Underground Network," Centre for Economic Performance, CEP Discussion Paper No. 1372, September 2015, http://cep.lse.ac.uk/pubs/download/dp1372.pdf.

or years to come! Instead, the key is to break the activity down into small steps, similar to how you did in creating an actionable plan, and then apply the learning loop to those small pieces. Notice that the tennis example wasn't "Do: Play a game. Assess: You won or lost." It was about improving one specific piece of the game: the serve. In the decision-making example, you might apply the learning loop to your ability to build a habit, or to counteract a certain bias, or to focus on satisficing instead of maximizing. So for the one category of "decision-making," you'll end up with loops within loops within loops, all contributing to small changes that add up to overall improvement.

As you move through the learning loop, here are some tips for success at each stage:

- Do: Make sure that you're conscious about what you're doing. In a way, your assessment should start while you're still doing. Remember that our memories can be funky, so you want to really pay attention in the moment, not just in hindsight.
- Assess: Don't equate bad outcomes with bad decisions/ actions, or good outcomes with good decisions/actions. Remember that everything is a bet, and luck and chance always play a role. Sometimes you can do everything right and still get a bad outcome. Maybe you hit a perfect serve, but a gust of wind knocks the ball off course. Or you can do everything wrong and manage to get really lucky. So try to assess your decisions and actions, not just outcomes.
- Get feedback: For feedback to be most effective, it needs to be timely, specific, and actionable. In the tennis serve example, say you got the feedback after practice instead of during practice. The next day, when you went to modify

your serve, you might not remember exactly how it felt the previous day when you were hitting long, so it would be more difficult for you to adjust to the right timing. Or imagine your boss told you, "You need to get better at communication." What are you supposed to do with that? It's too vague for you to know how to modify your behavior. If your boss instead said, "When making requests, you often fail to include a timeline for completion," that's specific and actionable—you know exactly what you need to do to improve your communication: include a timeline.

- Modify: The "do less, then obsess" principle applies here too. You'll likely have multiple loops running at any given time, which is fine. For instance, if you're working on improving your tennis game, you might work on both your serve and your backhand. But try not to modify too many things at once within each individual loop. So in working on your serve, you don't want to change your racket, your grip, your toss, your stance, and your timing all at once from one serve to the next. You're better off looping and fine-tuning just a couple of things before moving on to the others.

When using the learning loop, remember that you can learn from both your successes and your failures. We have a tendency to focus on just the bad outcomes (like surgeons do in M&M conferences), but it's important to also look at your good outcomes, so you can figure out what you did right, or whether you just got lucky.

No matter how skilled you are at something, you always have room for growth. So the learning loop can and should be a constant part of your life.

MEASURE YOUR PROGRESS AND CELEBRATE ALONG THE WAY

With career and life goals, the finish line can be so far away that it's hard to tell when we're making progress. You can put in a ton of time and effort without feeling like you're getting any closer to your goals, which can be demotivating. The good news is that most of the time, you *are* making progress. You just need to find a way to measure it so you can see it. And bonus: the more you can see your progress, the more progress you make!

One study about the importance of measuring progress was done with exercise.[54] The participants all performed a baseline session on exercise bikes. Then they did additional sessions after being split into four groups: a control group that got no further instruction, a group that was given a goal (increase output on the bike 40 percent relative to the first session), a group that was given performance feedback during the sessions, and a group that was given both a goal and performance feedback. The groups that were given either a goal or feedback, but not both, increased their output slightly more than the control group. The group that was given both a goal and feedback more than *doubled* the improvement of any of the other groups.

It's not just exercise either. Feedback on progress is also important to more complex and less easily measured goals. Another study done with social workers showed that outcomes improved if the social workers were given feedback about what ended up happening with their cases, even though

---

54   A. Bandura and D Cervone, "Self-Evaluative and Self-Efficacy Mechanisms Governing the Motivational Effects of Goal Systems," *Journal of Personality and Social Psychology* 45, no. 5 (1983): 1017–28.

some of those outcomes didn't occur until months down the line.[55]

~~~

The more you understand where you are in relation to your goal—both the progress you've made and the distance you have to go—the better your performance will be.

~~~

You can often easily track progress in a journal or various apps, especially when your goals have numbers attached to them, like many financial or fitness goals. Even if you don't have a number to track, basically any goal can be measured in relation to the smaller, mid-level goals you complete on the way to the big goal.

As you measure your progress and start to hit important milestones, take the time to celebrate! You don't need to slog away for years before getting a payoff. Give yourself rewards along the way, and be proud of the work you're doing.

BUILD A TEAM TO SUPPORT YOU

Very few great achievements are accomplished alone. Even a cyclist who wins the Tour de France (a seemingly individual accomplishment) has an entire team supporting them—team-mates to allow for drafting, coaches to help with training,

---

55   Service and Gallagher, *Think Small.*

support staff to manage logistics, and so on. Having your own team to support you is one of the best ways to ensure long-term success.

As discussed in the previous chapter, you can partner up with someone pursuing a similar (or even a completely different) goal as you, and you can also join support groups or relevant organizations. These people and groups are your teammates—the ones who will put in the work beside you. You can also recruit your family, friends, or colleagues to help you stay committed. These are your support staff, the people metaphorically providing you water and food along the race so you can keep going.

The last key member of your support team is a coach. Your coach could be a domain-specific teacher or mentor, like a personal fitness trainer, language teacher, or leadership coach. They could also be a more general life coach, whose job is to keep you on track toward your goals, whatever they may be. Both psychology and human performance research show coaching to improve goal attainment, reduce stress, increase resilience, and improve both hope and well-being.[56] I've personally used all types of coaches and find both incredibly helpful. My guitar teacher gives me structured lessons and detailed feedback, helping me progress more quickly. Mentors in medicine have helped me become not just a better surgeon but a better person. Having a life coach has helped

---

56 A. M. Grant, L. S. Green, and J. Rynsaardt, "Developmental Coaching for High School Teachers: Executive Coaching Goes to School," *Consulting Psychology Journal: Practice and Research* 62, no. 3 (2010): 151–68; Gordon B. Spence, Michael J. Cavanagh, and Anthony M. Grant (2008), "The Integration of Mindfulness Training and Health Coaching: An Exploratory Study," *Coaching: An International Journal of Theory, Research and Practice* 1, no. 2 (2008): 145–63; L. S. Green, L. G. Oades, and A.M. Grant, "Cognitive-Behavioral, Solution-Focused Life Coaching: Enhancing Goal Striving, Well-Being, and Hope," *Journal of Positive Psychology* 1, no. 3 (2006): 142–49.

me be more productive and more successful all across my life, while being happier, more joyful, and less stressed along the way.

Coaches can provide a lot of value in different ways. They offer an outside perspective, which is a good way to avoid a lot of the biases that come up in decision-making. A good coach will challenge you on your status quo bias and sunk cost fallacies because they don't have a vested interest in what you've done up to the current point; they're only interested in helping you build your best future. They can help you create an actionable plan and adapt it in response to changing circumstances. They can help identify and track the gap between where you are and where you want to be and can help you measure your progress. A good coach will also provide feedback and hold you accountable, helping you stay committed and on track toward your goals. I've definitely had times where I didn't feel the motivation to work toward a goal but forced myself to anyway, just because I knew my coach would ask me about it at our next session. A coach will help you with everything in this book and more, but on a far more personalized level, they'll identify and help you follow through on the strategies that work best for *you*.

Some people think coaching is not accessible to them, assuming it will be too expensive or that finding the right coach will be too difficult, but I encourage you to try. It has surprised me and many I have recommended coaching to how easy it was to find a good coach. And the personal stories match the research: coaching is incredibly helpful. In choosing a coach, you should find somebody you trust and you relate to. At the end of the day, having a coach is having a relationship. You shouldn't have to pay to get an introductory call, and if you do, that's a red flag. Your coach should be able to tell you their own experience of having a coach. If they don't believe in coaching enough to have had one of their own or they think they have nothing left to learn in life, those are red flags too! And you should enjoy the experience. Coaching may not always be comfortable, but it should be rewarding. The two of you need to be a good fit. It's either a "Hell yes!" for both of you, or it's a no. And when you find one who is a "Hell yes!" for you, you've added a powerful member to your support team—someone whose expertise is in helping you achieve your goals.

You can accomplish a lot on your own, but you can accomplish even more with help, so take advantage of support that's out there for you!

KEEP GROWING!

Accomplishing big goals isn't always easy. You're going to face challenges and doubt your decisions. And you're going to make mistakes. That's okay! As long as you keep learning and growing, you will keep making progress, and that's really the point. You wouldn't want a surgeon whose education stopped once they graduated medical school. You want the surgeon who does the M&M conferences and is constantly trying to get better and improve outcomes. The same is true for you. You can learn from every decision and outcome, both good and bad, and continue to improve throughout life.

So remember your growth mindset and get gritty, persevering with passion. Do less, then obsess. Use the learning loop. Measure your progress and celebrate your wins. Build a team to support you. And no matter what, keep growing.

CONCLUSION

Just choices. They measure the distance between who we are and who we're turning into.

—AMBELIN KWAYMULLINA AND EZEKIEL KWAYMULLINA, *THE THINGS SHE'S SEEN*

What shirt to wear, what to do this weekend, the freelance gig or the office job—you have the tools now to make decisions like these and any other in your life. You might still be in the metaphorical jungle, only able to see a short distance in front of you, but now you have a compass and a map. You've gotten the lay of the land, and you can begin carving your own path forward. You will face obstacles. Biases will crop up and try to keep you on the comfortable, easy path, even if it's not headed the right direction, or they may pull you down distracting side trails. But as long as you know your goals and are committed to achieving them, you don't have to feel lost. You may need to climb over or around barriers, cut through dense vegetation, or swim across rivers, but with persistence, you will continue to make progress.

I know we've covered a lot, so let's do a final recap of the most important lessons:

You have no destiny. You have choices. Because the future is uncertain, every choice is a bet. But by using the strategies and tips outlined in this book, you can make smarter bets and come out ahead more often.

Cultivate a growth mindset. Your talent, skills, and personality are not set in stone. You always have the opportunity to change, learn, and grow.

Not making a choice is still a decision—and typically not a very good one. You're always making choices, even if it seems like you're not. Choosing to do nothing or to make no changes means betting your health, wealth, and happiness on the default option. Don't miss out on amazing opportunities simply because of a fear to decide. Be conscious about your choices.

Beware your biases. The sunk cost fallacy, the status quo bias, the distinction bias, the peak–end rule, hedonic adaptation, time discounting, the exponential growth bias—these biases are unconscious and instinctual. In many scenarios, they serve us well, but rarely do one-size-fits-all rules *always* work. Be aware of your biases and try not to let them sway you from the path you actually want to be on.

Take the time to figure out the big stuff—your long-term goals. Without a destination in mind, you'll never reach it. You have only this one life to live. Make it one you love by working toward the things that will bring you happiness and well-being. Keep in mind the five factors that are scientifically proven to bring us the most happiness: social connection, health and activity, curiosity, learning, and giving.

Use a process for decision-making. With a process, you can counteract your biases, and the structure will help you fine-tune and improve your decision-making.

Focus on your true top-level goals. Everything comes with an opportunity cost. You can only do so many things at once, so focus on a few, truly top-level goals in your life. Do less, then obsess.

Create an actionable plan. Some goals can feel overwhelming in their complexity and scope. But you don't need to do everything today. You just need to take *one step*. Keep taking steps every day, and the compound effects will add up. Create an actionable plan by breaking your big goal down into small, easily manageable steps.

Build good habits. Time and energy are limited resources. Make the most of both by building habits that support progress toward your goals. The more actions you can put on autopilot, the faster and easier it will be to achieve your goals. Use your understanding of the habit loop—cue, behavior, reward—to build long-term habits that stick. Remember to start small, then you can stack your habits as high as you need to.

Stay committed. It's going to be a long journey toward achieving your biggest goals. You will need commitment. Fortunately, commitment isn't just an innate skill you're good or bad at. It's something you build. Keep yourself on track by making your commitment public, using rewards, and when helpful, putting something at stake. Build and lean on your support team.

Keep practicing and learning. Achieving meaningful goals is a pursuit that never ends. You may achieve individual goals, but new ones will take their place. So get gritty. Cultivate perseverance and passion, becoming a lifelong learner.

For the final time (in this book—not in your life), I want you to imagine your future self. Imagine that you've followed all this advice, and you've accomplished all of your current goals. Imagine what has changed. Your career? Your hobbies? Your relationships? Your living situation? Everything?

It's time to start building that future. Today. Not tomorrow, not a week or year from now, *today.* If you're feeling overwhelmed, uncertain where to begin, or like you need some additional help or guidance, check out my website, fredericbahnson.com, for more exercises and resources. Otherwise, start applying the advice from this book. These tips and strategies are backed by both science and experience, and they work, but only if you actually put them into practice. So just do it. Pick one thing and try it out. Decide today to build the life you want.

ACKNOWLEDGMENTS

As I have mentioned in this book, memory is an imprecise and incomplete thing. I will begin these acknowledgments with that, and a general statement of gratitude that I have learned from, been mentored or supported by, and in general benefitted from more people than I am capable of naming. This work has been the effort of a team that has helped me organize and articulate these stories and ideas far more coherently than I might have done on my own. And the ideas themselves are not mine, really, but my gathering and interpretation of the work and thoughts of so many others. They are the giants at whose feet I sit.

In (relative) particular, I must acknowledge the work of every author and researcher (and the teams that support them) listed in the references and recommended resources in this book. It is their work that has improved my own and that I strive to enact and share. I also have specific thanks to Kelsey Adams and the whole team at Scribe Media, including Michael Nagin, Cristina Ricci, and Sarafina Riskind, who together took a rough manuscript and turned it into a well-polished book. If you've found the ideas here useful, your thanks can go to the researchers and writers before me, whose teaching and knowledge have guided me in bringing these things together. And if you've found this understandable, or even enjoyable to read, you have Kelsey to thank.

I have unending gratitude to my parents, Robert and Debbie, who taught me from the start that what others see as important is often a lot different from what we see as fulfilling, and who encouraged and taught me to see the world and my place in it as a grand adventure, filled with opportunities for learning and wonder. What I have learned from them is the foundation of all I have tried, learned, overcome, become, and created.

And of course, this work is due in large part to my wife, Margarita, and our two daughters, Cecilia and Penelope. It is Margarita's belief in me and her encouragement and patience that have supported and fueled both the learning that became this book and the work of creating the book itself. And it is for the future embodied in our daughters and the inspiring ways they approach that future that I hope this work can help more people confidently make the decisions that matter to them and follow through on those decisions for the benefit of themselves and all around them.

ABOUT THE AUTHOR

DR. FREDERIC BAHNSON is a personal and executive coach who works with individuals and teams to help them achieve their goals—from productivity to balance to happiness. He has spent two decades studying and translating the art and science of decision-making into practical strategies that can improve his clients' performance and well-being. He has consulted for and coached tech founders, healthcare executives, students, government officials, teachers and school directors, doctors, and other professionals.

Frederic holds a bachelor's in physics from Reed College and worked as a systems engineer before deciding to pursue medicine. He earned his medical degree from Oregon Health & Science University, and he completed his five years of general surgery training at Santa Barbara Cottage Hospital, with experience in trauma at LA County Hospital in Los Angeles. He has also served as a startup advisor and Chief Medical Officer for Macro-Eyes, an AI company focused on global public health and multiple-time winner of Gates Foundation Global Grand Challenges. For his healthcare system, Frederic has served as Chief of the Department of Surgery at Samaritan Albany General Hospital and a Medical Director for data analytics in addition to continuing to practice as a general surgeon. Along the way, he has won several awards for teaching and mentoring, in addition to enjoying the inherent rewards of coaching.

Frederic lives in Oregon with his wife, two daughters, and their dogs. His favorite activity is learning, and he enjoys exploration of any kind, from spending time on local trails with his family to meeting new people and discovering new perspectives. Frederic has built a balanced and successful life with time for trail ultramarathons and obstacle course runs along with family time, guitar lessons, travel, and all his professional pursuits. His goal is to create immediate impact with sustainable change and life-changing results. If you want to connect with him about coaching you or your team toward your most meaningful goals, you can reach him through his website, fredericbahnson.com.

44378151R00163